ZIML Math Competition Book

Division E 2018-2019

Areteem Institute

ZIML Math Competition Book Division E 2018-19

Edited by   John Lensmire
            David Reynoso
            Kevin Wang
            Kelly Ren

Copyright © 2019 ARETEEM INSTITUTE

WWW.ARETEEM.ORG

PUBLISHED BY ARETEEM PRESS

ALL RIGHTS RESERVED. No part of this publication may be reproduced, stored in a retrieval system, or transmitted, in any form or by any means, electronic, mechanical, photocopying, recording, or otherwise, without prior written permission of the publisher, except for "fair use" or other noncommercial uses as defined in Sections 107 and 108 of the U.S. Copyright Act.

ISBN-10: 1-944863-44-3
ISBN-13: 978-1-944863-44-9

First printing, July 2019.

TITLES PUBLISHED BY ARETEEM PRESS

Cracking the High School Math Competitions (and Solutions Manual) - Covering AMC 10 & 12, ARML, and ZIML
Mathematical Wisdom in Everyday Life (and Solutions Manual) - From Common Core to Math Competitions
Geometry Problem Solving for Middle School (and Solutions Manual) - From Common Core to Math Competitions
Fun Math Problem Solving For Elementary School (and Solutions Manual)

ZIML MATH COMPETITION BOOK SERIES

ZIML Math Competition Book Division E 2016-2017
ZIML Math Competition Book Division M 2016-2017
ZIML Math Competition Book Division H 2016-2017
ZIML Math Competition Book Jr Varsity 2016-2017
ZIML Math Competition Book Varsity Division 2016-2017
ZIML Math Competition Book Division E 2017-2018
ZIML Math Competition Book Division M 2017-2018
ZIML Math Competition Book Division H 2017-2018
ZIML Math Competition Book Jr Varsity 2017-2018
ZIML Math Competition Book Varsity Division 2017-2018
ZIML Math Competition Book Division E 2018-2019
ZIML Math Competition Book Division M 2018-2019
ZIML Math Competition Book Division H 2018-2019
ZIML Math Competition Book Jr Varsity 2018-2019
ZIML Math Competition Book Varsity Division 2018-2019

MATH CHALLENGE CURRICULUM TEXTBOOKS SERIES

Math Challenge I-A Pre-Algebra and Word Problems
Math Challenge I-B Pre-Algebra and Word Problems
Math Challenge I-C Algebra
Math Challenge II-A Algebra
Math Challenge II-B Algebra
Math Challenge III Algebra

Math Challenge I-A Geometry
Math Challenge I-B Geometry
Math Challenge I-C Topics in Algebra
Math Challenge II-A Geometry
Math Challenge II-B Geometry
Math Challenge III Geometry
Math Challenge I-A Counting and Probability
Math Challenge I-B Counting and Probability
Math Challenge I-C Geometry
Math Challenge II-A Combinatorics
Math Challenge II-B Combinatorics
Math Challenge III Combinatorics
Math Challenge I-A Number Theory
Math Challenge I-B Number Theory
Math Challenge I-C Finite Math
Math Challenge II-A Number Theory
Math Challenge II-B Number Theory
Math Challenge III Number Theory

COMING SOON FROM ARETEEM PRESS

Fun Math Problem Solving For Elementary School Vol. 2 (and Solutions Manual)
Counting & Probability for Middle School (and Solutions Manual) - From Common Core to Math Competitions
Number Theory Problem Solving for Middle School (and Solutions Manual) - From Common Core to Math Competitions

The books are available in paperback and eBook formats (including Kindle and other formats).
To order the books, visit https://areteem.org/bookstore.

Contents

Introduction 7

1 ZIML Contests 15
1.1 October 2018 17
1.2 November 2018 25
1.3 December 2018 35
1.4 January 2019 43
1.5 February 2019 51
1.6 March 2019 59
1.7 April 2019 67
1.8 May 2019 75
1.9 June 2019 85

2 ZIML Solutions 93
2.1 October 2018 94
2.2 November 2018 100
2.3 December 2018 108
2.4 January 2019 116
2.5 February 2019 123

Copyright © ARETEEM INSTITUTE. All rights reserved.

2.6	March 2019	131
2.7	April 2019	139
2.8	May 2019	146
2.9	June 2019	154
3	**Appendix**	**161**
3.1	Division E Topics Covered	161
3.2	Glossary of Common Math Terms	163
3.3	ZIML Answers	170

Introduction

Each month during the school year, Areteem Institute hosts the online Zoom International Math League (ZIML) competitions. Students can compete in one of five divisions based on their age and mathematical level (details shown on Page 9).

This book contains the problems, answers, and full solutions from the nine ZIML Division E Competitions held during the 2018-2019 School Year. It is divided into three parts:

1. The complete Division E ZIML Competitions (20 questions per competition) from October 2018 to June 2019.
2. The solutions for each of the competitions, including detailed work and helpful tricks.
3. An appendix including the topics and knowledge points covered for Division E, a glossary including common mathematical terms, and answer keys for each of the competitions so students can easily check their work.

The questions found on the ZIML competitions are meant to test your problem solving skills and train you to apply the knowledge you know to many different applications. We hope you enjoy the problems!

About Zoom International Math League

The Zoom International Math League (ZIML) has a simple goal: provide a platform for students to build and share their passion for math and other STEM fields with students from around the globe. Started in 2008 as the Southern California Mathematical Olympiad, ZIML has a rich history of past participants who have advanced to top tier colleges and prestigious math competitions, including American Math Competitions, MATHCOUNTS, and the International Math Olympaid.

The ZIML Core Online Programs, most available with a free account at `ziml.areteem.org`, include:

- **Daily Magic Spells:** Provides a problem a day (Monday through Friday) for students to practice, with full solutions available the next day.
- **Weekly Brain Potions:** Provides one problem per week posted in the online discussion forum at `ziml.areteem.org`. Usually the problem does not have a simple answer, and students can join the discussion to share their thoughts regarding the scenarios described in the problem, explore the math concepts behind the problem, give solutions, and also ask further questions.
- **Monthly Contests:** The ZIML Monthly Contests are held the first weekend of each month during the school year (October through June). Students can compete in one of 5 divisions to test their knowledge and determine their strengths and weaknesses, with winners announced after the competition.
- **Math Competition Practice:** The Practice page contains sample ZIML contests and an archive of AMC-series tests for online practice. The practices simulate the real contest environment with time-limits of the contests automatically controlled by the server.
- **Online Discussion Forum:** The Online Discussion Forum

Introduction

is open for any comments and questions. Other discussions, such as hard Daily Magic Spells or the Weekly Brain Potions are also posted here.

These programs encourage students to participate consistently, so they can track their progress and improvement each year.

In addition to the online programs, ZIML also hosts onsite Local Tournaments and Workshops in various locations in the United States. Each summer, there are onsite ZIML Competitions at held at Areteem Summer Programs, including the International ZIML Convention, which is a two day convention with one day of workshops and one day of competition.

ZIML Monthly Contests are organized into five divisions ranging from upper elementary school to advanced material based on high school math.

- **Varsity:** This is the top division. It covers material on the level of the last 10 questions on the AMC 12 and AIME level. This division is open to all age levels.
- **Junior Varsity:** This is the second highest competition division. It covers material at the AMC 10/12 level and State and National MathCounts level. This division is open to all age levels.
- **Division H:** This division focuses on material from a standard high school curriculum. It covers topics up to and including pre-calculus. This division will serve as excellent practice for students preparing for the math portions of the SAT or ACT. This division is open to all age levels.
- **Division M:** This division focuses on problem solving using math concepts from a standard middle school math curriculum. It covers material at the level of AMC 8 and School or Chapter MathCounts. This division is open to all students who have not started grade 9.

Introduction

- **Division E:** This division focuses on advanced problem solving with mathematical concepts from upper elementary school. It covers material at a level comparable to MOEMS Division E. This division is open to all students who have not started grade 6.

This problem book features the Division E Contests. For a detailed list of topics covered for Division E see p.161 in the Appendix.

To participate in the ZIML Online Programs, create a free account at `ziml.areteem.org`. The ZIML site features are also provided on the ZIML Mobile App, which is available for download from Apple's App Store and Google Play Store.

About Areteem Institute

Areteem Institute is an educational institution that develops and provides in-depth and advanced math and science programs for K-12 (Elementary School, Middle School, and High School) students and teachers. Areteem programs are accredited supplementary programs by the Western Association of Schools and Colleges (WASC). Students may attend the Areteem Institute in one or more of the following options:

- Live and real-time face-to-face online classes with audio, video, interactive online whiteboard, and text chatting capabilities;
- Self-paced classes by watching the recordings of the live classes;
- Short video courses for trending math, science, technology, engineering, English, and social studies topics;
- Summer Intensive Camps held on prestigious university campuses and Winter Boot Camps;
- Practice with selected free daily problems and monthly ZIML competitions at `ziml.areteem.org`.

Areteem courses are designed and developed by educational experts and industry professionals to bring real world applications into STEM education. The programs are ideal for students who wish to build their mathematical strength in order to excel academically and eventually win in Math Competitions (AMC, AIME, USAMO, IMO, ARML, MathCounts, Math Olympiad, ZIML, and other math leagues and tournaments, etc.), Science Fairs (County Science Fairs, State Science Fairs, national programs like Intel Science and Engineering Fair, etc.) and Science Olympiads, or for students who purely want to enrich their academic lives by taking more challenging courses and developing outstanding analytical, logical, and creative problem solving skills.

Since 2004 Areteem Institute has been teaching with methodology that is highly promoted by the new Common Core State Standards: stressing the conceptual level understanding of the math concepts, problem solving techniques, and solving problems with real world applications. With the guidance from experienced and passionate professors, students are motivated to explore concepts deeper by identifying an interesting problem, researching it, analyzing it, and using a critical thinking approach to come up with multiple solutions.

Thousands of math students who have been trained at Areteem have achieved top honors and earned top awards in major national and international math competitions, including Gold Medalists in the International Math Olympiad (IMO), top winners and qualifiers at the USA Math Olympiad (USAMO/JMO) and AIME, top winners at the Zoom International Math League (ZIML), and top winners at the MathCounts National Competition. Many Areteem Alumni have graduated from high school and gone on to enter their dream colleges such as MIT, Cal Tech, Harvard, Stanford, Yale, Princeton, U Penn, Harvey Mudd College, UC Berkeley, or UCLA. Those who have graduated from colleges are now playing important roles in their fields of endeavor.

Further information about Areteem Institute, as well as updates and errata of this book, can be found online at `http://www.areteem.org`.

Acknowledgments

This book contains the Online ZIML Division E Problems from the 2018-19 school year. These problems were created and compiled by the staff of Areteem Institute. These problems were inspired by questions from the Areteem Math Challenge Courses, past questions on the ACT/SAT/GRE, past math competitions, math textbooks, and countless other resources and people encountered by the Areteem Curriculum Department in their life devoted to math. We thank all these sources for growing and nurturing our passion for math.

The Areteem staff, including John Lensmire, David Reynoso, Kevin Wang, and Kelly Ren, are the main contributors who compiled, edited, and reviewed this book.

Lastly, thanks to all the students who have participated and continue to participate in the Zoom International Math League. Your dedication to the Daily Magic Spells and Monthly Contests makes all of this possible, and we hope you continue to enjoy ZIML for years to come!

1. ZIML Contests

This part of the book contains the Division E ZIML Contests from the 2018-19 School Year. There were nine monthly competitions, held on the dates found below:

- October 5-7
- November 2-4
- December 7-9
- January 4-6
- February 1-3
- March 1-3
- April 5-7
- May 3-5
- June 7-9

1.1 ZIML October 2018 Division E

Below are the 20 Problems from the Division E ZIML Competition held in October 2018.
The answer key is available on p.170 in the Appendix.
Full solutions to these questions are available starting on p.94.

Problem 1
A 4-digit number has 2 more ones than tens, twice as many thousands as tens, three times as many hundreds as ones. If the number has no repeated digits, what is the number?

Problem 2
How many triangles are there in the diagram below?

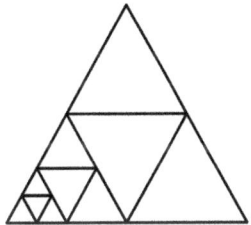

Problem 3
What is the next number in the following sequence?

$$2, 6, 7, 21, 22, 66, 67, \ldots$$

Problem 4
Gregory drew two squares to form a new figure, like in the diagram below.

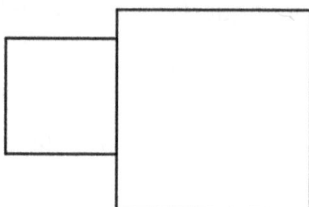

If the perimeter of the small square is 16 and the perimeter of the larger square is 28, what is the perimeter of the figure?

Problem 5
In Clementine's swimming class, 3 out of every 7 students wear green swimming caps. If there are 18 students wearing green swimming caps, how many students are there in Clementine's class?

Problem 6
Eric is 5 years older than his brother. 2 years ago Eric's age was twice his brother's. How old is Eric's brother today?

Problem 7

Tommy and Larry are having a toy car race. Tommy's car can travel 1.5 meters per second. Larry's car can travel 1.3 meters per second. Since Tommy's car is faster, they agree to give Larry a 2 second head start. If the track is 39 meters long, how many seconds will there be between the times when the winning and losing cars cross the finish line?

Problem 8

Gemma built a house with a square piece of paper and a triangular piece of paper, like in the diagram below:

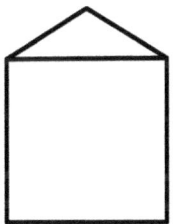

If the base of the house is 10 cm long and the full height of the house is 13 cm, how many square centimeters is the total area of the pieces of paper Gemma used to build the house?

Problem 9

Aaron bought a jacket at a discount store. The jacket had a tag price of $49 and used a coupon for a discount of 30% off the tag price. What was the jacket's discounted price? Give your answer in dollars rounded to the nearest cent.

Problem 10
In the city of Wet Winds it rains every three days, and there are huge gusts of wind every other day. Today it rained and there were huge gusts of wind. How many times will there be rain and huge gusts of wind on the same day during the following 4 weeks?

Problem 11
Christy needs to type an essay with at least 500 words for her English class. She can type, on average, 44 words per minute. At this rate, how many whole minutes would Christy need to type enough words for her essay?

Problem 12
Manny will fence a rectangular yard that is three times as long as it is wide. If his yard has an area of 75 square yards, how many linear yards of fence will he need?

Problem 13
Annabel is picking out colors to paint her old car. She will either paint the car using only tones from a green color palette or using only tones of from a blue color palette. She decided to use one tone for the doors, another tone for the hood and a third tone for the rest of the car. The green color palette has 4 different tones of green while the blue color palette has 5 tones of blue. In how many ways can she paint her car?

Problem 14

Jayne served 104 ounces of juice in 11 cups. She has some 8-ounce cups and some 12-ounce cups. If she used all of her cups and served all the juice she had, how many 8-ounce cups did she serve?

Problem 15

Ms. Tammy asked her students to draw in a piece of paper a triangle that is similar to the one she drew on the board (see picture).

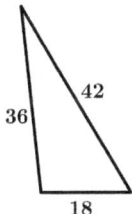

Candace was able to draw a similar triangle. The two shortest sides of Candace's triangle measured 6 cm and 12 cm. How many centimeters is the length of the third side of Candace's triangle?

Problem 16
Lola was playing with some wooden cubes at home. Currently all of her cubes are in a corner of the room like in the diagram below.

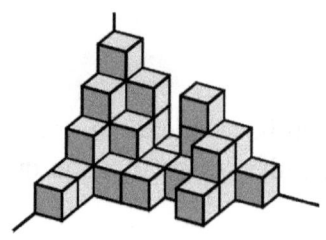

Using the cubes she has, Lola wants to build the largest cube she can. How many wooden cubes would she need to build the biggest cube she can make?

Problem 17
A list of numbers in arithmetic progression starts with 19 and ends in 107. If there are 9 numbers in the list, what is the number in the middle?

Problem 18
Marcie went to the ice cream shop with her mom. She couldn't decide what to get, so she told the ice cream guy to randomly pick two different flavors from chocolate chip, mint-chocolate, pecan nut, coffee, and chocolate-strawberry, and give her one scoop of each in a cone. The probability that her ice cream contains no chocolate is $P\%$. What is P? Round your answer to the nearest tenth.

Problem 19

Super strong ants are a species of ants that can carry up to 150 times their own weight. Duncan, a super strong ant, was able to lift an object that weighs 40 grams, but not an object that weights 40.01 grams. What is Duncan's weight? Give your answer in grams rounded to the nearest hundredth.

Problem 20

There are three buckets in the patio. One is shaped like a cube and has side length 30 inches. The other two are shaped like prisms with square bases of side 40 inches and a height 60 inches. How many cubic inches of water can all three buckets hold together?

1.2 ZIML November 2018 Division E

Below are the 20 Problems from the Division E ZIML Competition held in November 2018.
The answer key is available on p.171 in the Appendix.
Full solutions to these questions are available starting on p.100.

Problem 1
Benjy bought one box of cans of dog food for his dog Petsy. The box comes with 3 layers of 15 cans each.

If Benjy paid $72 for the box, how many dollars did he pay for each can? Round your answer to the nearest cent.

Problem 2
Carter has a bag of candy that he wants to share with his friends. He gave 3 candies to each of his 7 friends, and was left with 5 candies for himself.

How many candies were originally in the bag?

Problem 3

After weeks of not doing any laundry, Ashton suddenly found himself with no clean clothes to wear, so he decided to wash all of his clothes.

He will need to wash and dry 5 full loads of clothes. There are 3 washing machines and 3 driers available for him to use. A washing machine takes 30 minutes to wash a load, and the drier takes 45 minutes to dry a load.

Assuming Ashton loads/unloads the washers and driers as soon as possible, how much time (in minutes) would he need to wash and dry all of his clothes?

Problem 4

Ivy used four congruent right triangles with side lengths of 5 inches, 12 inches, and 13 inches to build a pinwheel-like figure shown in the diagram below.

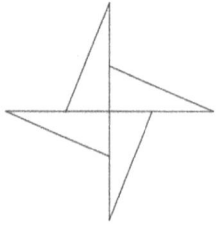

What is the perimeter of Ivy's figure in inches?

Problem 5
It takes Valerie 25 minutes to write a 500-word essay.

At this rate, how many words could Valerie write in 1 hour? Round your answer to the nearest integer.

Problem 6
In the following diagram $\angle A = 75°$, $\angle B = 55°$ and $\angle C = 45°$.

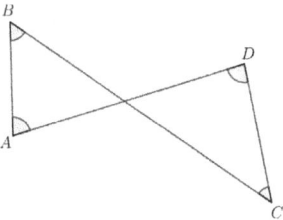

How many degrees is $\angle D$?

Problem 7
Janene and Dannie run on a circular track during sports class. Janene can complete one lap around the track in 5 minutes. Dannie can complete one lap around the track in 7 minutes.

They start running from the same place at the same time, and stop running when they are both at the finish line at the same time.

How many combined laps did Janene and Dannie run in total?

Problem 8

Rex plans to paint the walls of his room. He wants to use a color that is a mix of blue and green, and found his favorite color when he mixed 2 cups of blue paint with 3 cups of green paint.

If Rex will need 8 gallons of paint to paint the whole room, how many gallons of green paint must he buy? Round your answer to the nearest tenth.

Problem 9

Kathie is making a diorama of her house and she wants to make sure everything is scaled properly.

Right now she is working on building the courtyard, which is in the shape of a trapezoid like the one on the diagram below.

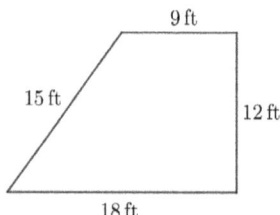

If she wants the shortest side of the trapezoid to be 10 cm long in her diorama, how many centimeters is the perimeter of the trapezoid in her diorama?

Problem 10

Patricia must form 4-digit numbers with no repeated digits using only the digits 0, 1, 2, 3, 7, or 9.

What is the difference between the smallest and the largest numbers Patricia can make?

Problem 11

Mr. Banks has been following closely the exchange rates between the US dollar (USD) and the Mexican Peso (MXN).

On Monday morning the exchange rate was 1 USD for 20 MXN. By the end of the week Mr. Banks noticed the exchange rate for 1 USD had increased by 3.2%.

After this increase, how many MXN is 1 USD? Round your answer to the nearest cent.

Problem 12

Three squares with side lengths 3, 4 and 5 overlap to form a new figure, like in the diagram below.

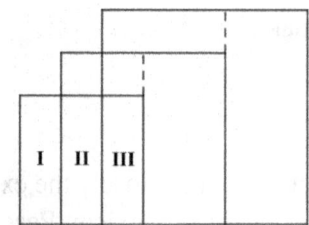

If the left sides of the two bigger squares divide the smaller square into three regions of equal size (labeled I, II, and III above), what is the area of the whole figure?

Problem 13

Kurtis has a deck of cards with 10 blue cards and 10 black cards. The blue cards and black cards are each numbered $1, \ldots, 10$.

If Kurtis randomly chooses one card, the probability that the card is a blue even number or a black multiple of 3 is $\dfrac{P}{Q}$ as a simplified fraction. What is $Q - P$?

Problem 14

Marissa needs to fence a portion of her yard to house some chicken. She wants to divide the yard in 5 sections, as pictured on the diagram below.

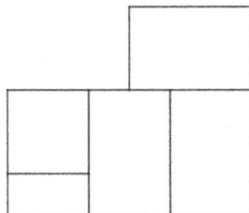

The three big rectangles are congruent, the width of the three big rectangles is the same as the side length of the square, and the width of the small rectangle is half of the side length of the square.

If she needs the square portion to have an area of 16 square yards, and she plans to fence all regions marked in her diagram, how many yards of fence will she need?

Problem 15

Ms. Webster was handing back some graded tests to her students when she realized she had lost Tamika's test.

To figure out Tamika's grade, she collected all tests again and calculated the average grade of the test, which was 81 points (not including Tamika's missing test). Ms. Webster remembers the average grade of all tests when she graded them was 82 points (including Tamika's).

If there are 17 total students in Ms. Webster's class, how many points did Tamika get on her test?

Problem 16

Mike has a bucket of water that can hold 5 gallons of water. He is using it to fill a tank that is in the shape of a rectangular prism with length 20 inches and width 10 inches.

After pouring 15 buckets full of water into the tank, how many inches high is the level of the water? Recall 1 gallon of water is equal to 231 cubic inches. Round your answer to the nearest inch.

Problem 17

The average speed of a common garden snail is 0.03 miles per hour.

What is their speed in inches per minute? Round your answer to the nearest tenth. (Recall 1 mi = 63360 in.)

Problem 18

Deena is visiting her favorite diner for lunch. She can choose between the lunch special or meals from the regular menu.

The lunch special includes: Caesar salad or soup of the day, one of three choices of the lunch special entrees, and one of two choices for dessert. (The lunch special entrees are NOT available on the regular menu.)

In the regular menu there are 4 choices for soup, 3 choices for salad, 6 entrees, and 4 desserts.

Deena will either go with the lunch special or she will order a soup, one entree, and one dessert. In how many different ways can she order lunch?

Problem 19

Clementine bought 15 bags of candy. Some bags had 100 candies, and some bags had 150 candies.

She poured all of the candies in a bowl, and counted 1950 candies in total.

How many bags of 100 candies did she buy?

Problem 20

Brian drew a portion of a pattern on a piece of paper, like the one in the diagram below.

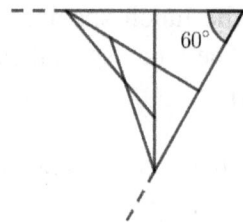

He then placed two mirrors over where the dotted lines are, producing a new figure when looking at the mirrors. This figure will consist of 6 identical copies of the diagram above, arranged in a circle.

How many lines of symmetry does this figure have? (Note: the dotted lines and the angle are not part of the pattern.)

1.3 ZIML December 2018 Division E

Below are the 20 Problems from the Division E ZIML Competition held in December 2018.
The answer key is available on p.172 in the Appendix.
Full solutions to these questions are available starting on p.108.

Problem 1
What is
$$10 \div 16 \times 50 \times 2 \div 15 \times 60$$
equal to?

Problem 2
Charlie has several boxes that contain 20 pounds of chocolate each.

He arranges the boxes to form a rectangular prism that is 5 boxes wide, 4 boxes long, and 3 boxes high.

Altogether, how many pounds of chocolate are there among all of these boxes that Charlie arranged?

Problem 3
Demetria just learned in school that hummingbirds can fly up to 45 miles per hour.

What is this speed in meters per second? Use the approximation $1\,\text{mi} = 1600\,\text{m}$. Round your answer to the nearest tenth.

Problem 4

Brant and Byron are making mini pizzas. They each start with a large amount of dough and split it into small balls of dough to make the mini pizzas.

Brant takes his dough and splits it in half, then splits the pieces in half again, then once more, and then one final time. Byron takes his dough and splits it in three, then splits the pieces in thirds again, and again one last time. (Note: in each step they split all the dough pieces they have.)

After both are done splitting their dough, how many small balls of dough do they have to make their mini pizzas?

Problem 5

In the following diagram, how many triangles do not contain the shaded triangle?

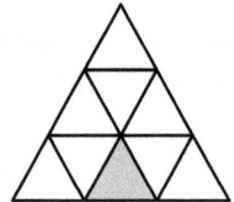

Problem 6

Dolores needs to buy mason jars and lids for her craft store. Surprisingly the mason jars and the lids are sold separately. Jars come in packs of 8 and lids come in packs of 20.

What is the least number of packs of lids she would need to buy so that she can have all jars with a lid, with no jars or lids left over?

Problem 7

Don is an expert juice maker. His specialty is an orange-carrot juice mix. To make 3 servings of juice, he mixes 2 cups of orange juice with 1 cup of carrot juice, he then blends it with 1 cup of diced celery and adds a few drops of super hot sauce. (Ignore the volume of a drop of hot sauce.)

Each serving of juice is P% orange juice. What is P? Round your answer to the nearest integer percent.

Problem 8

What is the next number in the sequence?

$$1, 2, 3, 4, 7, 8, 15, 16, 31, 32, \ldots$$

Problem 9

Jonathan just bought a board game that comes with a die. Jonathan suspects that the die is rigged so he tested it 100 times and kept record of the numbers he got:

Number	Frequency
1	15
2	15
3	16
4	25
5	19
6	10

According to the data in the table, the probability that Jonathan gets an odd number is $P\%$. What is P?

Problem 10

Kimberly drew a triangle with sides 10, 24 and 26, and a smaller similar triangle whose smallest side has length 5, as pictured in the diagram below.

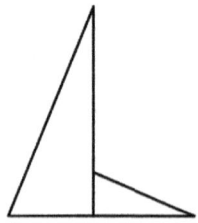

What is the perimeter of Kimberly's figure?

Problem 11

Lindsey has been collecting the sauce packets she gets with her food at fast food restaurants.

She has 12 more packets of Fire sauce than Hot sauce, and she has 116 sauce packs altogether.

How many packs of Fire sauce does she have?

Problem 12

In the following diagram there are squares of three different sizes.

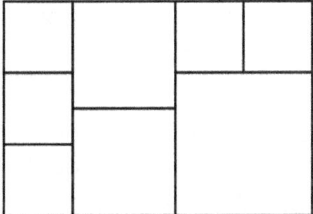

All squares have integer side lengths and form a rectangle that has width 12. (Here the width is the smaller dimension of the rectangle.)

What is the area of the whole rectangle?

Problem 13

Sally, the ant, likes traveling along the edges of a toy cube. Currently she is in the middle of an edge.

If Sally only walks over the edges of the cube what is the maximum number of edges she can visit before she visits the same vertex twice?

Problem 14

Cristy is decorating cupcakes with frosting. She knows she has enough frosting to "draw" a continuous line of frosting that is 3 meters long.

She wants to decorate each cupcake around the edge with a circle of frosting.

If each of the cupcakes has a diameter of 5 centimeters, how many cupcakes will she be able to decorate completely before she runs out of frosting? For this problem, use the approximation $\pi \approx \frac{22}{7}$.

Problem 15

Kasey's dog, Paul, loves milk. If Kasey gave him $2\frac{1}{4}$ gallons of milk, he'd finish it in 25 minutes.

Kasey knows she should not give Paul this much milk, so she only gives Paul one quart of milk each morning. How many minutes would Paul need to drink his milk every morning? Round your answer to the nearest integer. Recall there are 4 quarts in 1 gallon.

1.3 ZIML December 2018 Division E

Problem 16

Ella is 15 meters away from her favorite tree in the park. She decided to jump her way to the tree. She will alternate first jumping 2 meters towards the tree and then 1 meter away from the tree.

How many jumps will it take Ella to get to reach her favorite tree?

Problem 17

Penelope and some of her friends sit around a circular table. Then they take turns counting numbers starting from 1, and they stop when someone counts 144.

If Penelope takes the first turn, and the same person that counted 44 also counted 51, what is the last number Penelope counted?

Problem 18

In the diagram below a hexagon is formed using several equilateral triangles of area 1.

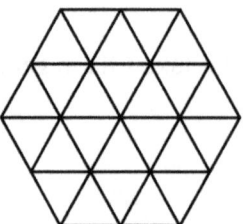

What is the area of the largest triangle that could be formed by rearranging the pieces that form the hexagon? (Note: you may not use all the pieces.)

Problem 19

Find the smallest 3-digit number that leaves a remainder of 7 when divided by 11 and a remainder of 4 when divided by 5

Problem 20

Call a number "funny" if it is divisible by its tens digit.

How many "funny" numbers are there between 100 and 160?

1.4 ZIML January 2019 Division E

Below are the 20 Problems from the Division E ZIML Competition held in January 2019.
The answer key is available on p.173 in the Appendix.
Full solutions to these questions are available starting on p.116.

Problem 1
Austin drew a triangle whose height is 5 times the length of its base. If the triangle has area 90, what is the length of the base of the triangle?

Problem 2
After Christmas Dante and four of his friends ate (altogether) as many candy canes as the smallest 3-digit number that can be formed with the digits 0, 2, 5, and 7 without repeating digits.

If each of the kids ate the same number of candy canes, how many candy canes did each of them eat?

Problem 3
Pablo and his dad have a pottery workshop. Pablo's dad can make four pots in the same time it takes Pablo to make three pots.

After working together for a few hours they made 63 pots in total. How many of those pots were made by Pablo?

Problem 4

In the following diagram the rectangles are twice as long as the side length of the big square, and the small squares have area 9.

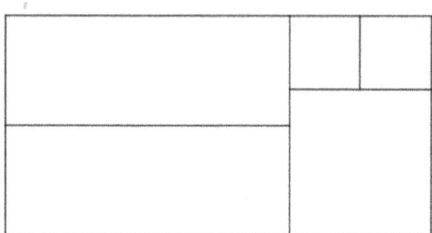

What is the area of the whole figure?

Problem 5

Adam, Bob and Charles pooled their money together to buy movie tickets and popcorn.

Adam had 2 more dollars than Bob, Bob had twice as much money as Charles, and Charles had 7 dollars. How many dollars did they have in total?

Problem 6
Consider the list of numbers

$$1, 2, 3, 5, 8, 13, 21, 34,$$

and find the average of this list.

If you randomly choose one number from the list, the probability you choose a number lower than the average can be written as $P\%$. What is P, rounded to the nearest tenth?

Problem 7
Robert needs to fence his yard which is in the shape of a rectangle with length 10 yards and width 18 yards. He also wants to divide the yard in four equal regions with a fence.

How many yards of fence is Robert going to need to fence the perimeter of the yard and divide it into four equal regions?

Problem 8
Multiply out all the factors of 60. How many zeros are at the end of this number?

Problem 9
Larry baked a pie and then cut it into 7 slices. Six of the slices were identical and the seventh was twice as big as the others.

If Larry measures the angle formed in the bigger slice, how many degrees would that angle be? Round your answer to the nearest degree.

Problem 10

Louise is a sales agent at a paper company. She gets an 8% commission on all sales she makes in a given week.

If this week she received a commission of $104, how many dollars did she sell?

Problem 11

The following diagram shows two similar triangles and the lengths of some of their sides.

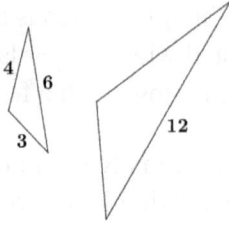

What is the perimeter of the big triangle?

Problem 12

Jessica's family exchanges presents every year after New Years. Each of the 6 members of the family buys a present and wraps it using a small box. All boxes are the same, so they have no way of knowing which present is which. Then one by one they open a present at random.

Jessica is the third person to open a present, and no one has picked yet the present she bought. The probability that she picks her own present is $P\%$. What is P? Round your answer to the nearest integer.

Problem 13

A right triangle is formed as in the diagram below

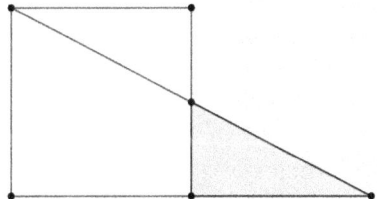

If the point shown on the edge of the square is the midpoint and the shaded triangle has area 4, what is the area of the square?

Problem 14

Lydia travels to school in her bike. The distance between her house and her school is 6 miles. If she takes 45 minutes to get to school, what is her average speed in miles per hour?

Problem 15

Tom has a box with an open top with length 15 cm, width 20 cm, and height 30 cm. He wants to cover all the exterior and the interior of the box with colored paper. How many square centimeters of colored paper will Tom need to cover the box?

Problem 16

Perry amazed his classmates by "doubling" a number on a calculator. He has his classmates type in any two-digit number, and after pressing some buttons Perry showed them their original number written twice in a row. For example, 25 became 2525 and 61 became 6161.

In fact, Perry was just multiplying the numbers by an integer K. What is K?

Problem 17

Trisha's mom just dropped her at school. Trisha decided to jump her way to the main door of the school. Every time she jumps, she jumps either 1 meter or 1.5 meters. The door is 18.5 meters away from her mom's car.

If Trisha jumped 15 times, how many times did she jump 1.5 meters?

1.4 ZIML January 2019 Division E

Problem 18

Stefan bought some packs of gum. He bought some mint flavored gum and some fruit flavored packs, 24 in total.

If Stefan bought 3 times as many fruit flavored packs as mint flavored packs, how many fruit flavored packs did he buy?

Problem 19

Jenna made a new friend who wanted to know her birthday. Jenna said that her birthday was in January, but that her friend would need to guess the day of the month with a few hints. Jenna told her that (i) her birthday was a perfect square, (ii) was in the second half of the month, and (iii) was not a multiple of 5. What day of the month is Jenna's birthday?

Problem 20

One large cube and two small congruent cubes are stacked as in the diagram below.

If the combined volume of all three cubes is 120, what is the volume of the large cube?

1.5 ZIML February 2019 Division E

Below are the 20 Problems from the Division E ZIML Competition held in February 2019.
The answer key is available on p.174 in the Appendix.
Full solutions to these questions are available starting on p.123.

Problem 1
Kallie is baking cookies. After she takes a tray of cookies from the oven, she needs to add some final decorations to each of the cookies.

Kallie has 8 trays of cookies, each with 5 rows of 7 cookies each.

If Kallie spends an average of 6 seconds decorating one cookie, how many minutes would she need to decorate all of her cookies? Round your answer to the nearest minute.

Problem 2
A rectangle is split into four rectangles as in the diagram below.

	12	
	16	10

The perimeters of three of the rectangles are 10, 12, 16, as labeled in the diagram.

What is the perimeter of the fourth rectangle?

Problem 3
Andy wants to line up his collection of toy soldiers. He has 8 different soldiers in total, 3 of which are special edition soldiers.

If he wants to line them up so so that the first and last soldiers are special edition soldiers, in how many different ways can he arrange his soldiers in line?

Problem 4
At Mr. Furn E. Ture's workshop, a team of 3 workers can assemble a dining table in 5 hours.

How many minutes would it take a crew of 5 workers to assemble a dining table?

Problem 5
Eddie bought a TV with a price tag of $800 (including tax). He bought it with a 15% off coupon and he will pay it in 12 monthly payments.

How many dollars will Eddie have to pay each month? Give your answer in dollars rounded to the nearest cent.

Problem 6
Meredith loves hats, and has tons of them. Looking at her collection of hats she realized she has 2 more baseball caps than three times the number of cowboy hats she has.

If in total she has 46 baseball caps and cowboy hats, how many cowboy hats does Meredith have?

Problem 7
Millie drew three equilateral triangles with different side lengths.

The first triangle had side length 5, the second triangle's side length was twice the side length of the first triangle, and the third triangle's side length was half of of the side length of the first triangle.

What is the combined perimeter of all three triangles?

Problem 8
How many diagonals does a regular undecagon have? (Recall an undecagon is a polygon with 11 sides).

Problem 9

At the dog park, Tris is in charge of keeping track of the number of small, large, and extra large dogs that visit.

This morning Tris noticed the ratio of small dogs to large dogs was 7 : 5, and the ratio of large dogs to extra large dogs was 3 : 1.

If there were more than 80 dogs at the dog park, but no more than 100, how many large dogs visited the park this morning?

Problem 10

Rita's fish tank is a rectangular prism that is 70 centimeters long, 40 centimeters wide, and 30 centimeters tall.

The faucet that she will use to fill the tank can pour 4 liters of water in one minute.

How many minutes would she need to fill her tank completely? (Recall that 1 liter is equal to 1000 cubic centimeters.)

Problem 11

Lance drew a regular pentagon with side length 4. He then drew a regular heptagon (seven sides) outside of the pentagon, sharing one side with the pentagon. Finally, he drew a regular nonagon (nine sides) sharing a side with the heptagon, making sure it did not overlap with the pentagon or the heptagon.

What is the perimeter of Lance's resulting figure?

Problem 12

Last night, it took Ally 40 minutes to drive from her office back home. Her average speed last night was 10 miles per hour slower than usual.

If her office is 26 miles away from her house, what is her usual average speed on her drive home from work? Round your answer to the nearest tenth.

Problem 13

Ms. Rosemary asked her students to draw two different triangles with the same area.

Dante drew one triangle with base 6 centimeters and height 14 centimeters.

If he wants his second triangle to have a height of 4 centimeters, how many centimeters should the length of its base be?

Problem 14

Lindsay was looking back at her recent candy purchases. Every day in December she bought 3 pieces of candy, and every day in January she bought twice as many pieces of candy as she did on a day in December.

How many pieces of candy did Lindsay buy during December and January?

Recall both December and January have 31 days.

Problem 15
Cecilia had a square piece of paper of 10 inches per side. She folded it diagonally in half, and then again. She then grabbed some scissors and cut a square piece of side length 2 inches out of her folded paper, making sure not to touch the edges of her paper as shown below.

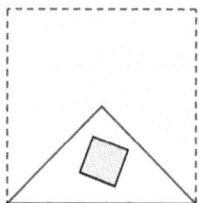

After making the cut, Cecilia unfolds her paper. What is the area (in square inches) of her paper now?

Problem 16
Ariel and Belle each made fair 4-sided die using clay in art class. Ariel labeled hers with the numbers $3, 4, 5, 6$ while Belle used the numbers $1, 2, 3, 4$.

If each roll their die, the probability that Ariel gets a number higher than Belle can be written as the reduced fraction $\frac{P}{Q}$. What is $P + Q$?

Problem 17

Lisa challenged her friends to guess the number she was thinking of. She gave them some clues to find it: (i) all four digits of the number are different, (ii) it has the digit 2 somewhere, (iii) the last digit is four times the first digit, and (iv) the second digit is three times the third digit.

Lisa did not realize that there was more than one number that could be found using her clues, so her friends guessed different numbers. What is the difference between the largest and the smallest numbers her friends could have found?

Problem 18

How many numbers from 1 to 200 (inclusive) have exactly one digit 0?

Problem 19

The third number in a geometric sequence is 63 and the fifth number is 567.

What is the second number in the sequence?

Problem 20

Lance wrote a sequence of numbers defined as follows: (i) if the last number he wrote is a multiple of 3, then the next number is 2 less than twice this number; (ii) if the last number he wrote is 1 more than a multiple of 3, then he adds 2 to this number; (iii) if the last number he wrote is 2 more than a multiple of 3, then the next number is 3 times this number.

If Lance started with the number 44, what is the 4th number he wrote?

1.6 ZIML March 2019 Division E

Below are the 20 Problems from the Division E ZIML Competition held in March 2019.
The answer key is available on p.175 in the Appendix.
Full solutions to these questions are available starting on p.131.

Problem 1
A fraction that is equivalent to $\frac{48}{80}$ is such that its numerator and denominator add up to 32. What is the denominator of the fraction?

Problem 2
Consider points A, B, C, and D on the number line.

If $AC = 7$, $BD = 7$, and $CD = 4$, what is the length of AD?

Problem 3
The sum of two numbers is 107 and their difference is 53.

What is the smaller of the two numbers?

Problem 4
The local park is famous for attracting lots of pigeons and doves. It is known by the locals that the ratio of pigeons to doves in the park is 3 : 5.

If there are currently 93 pigeons, how many pigeons and doves are there in the park?

Problem 5
In the following diagram the grid is made out of unit squares.

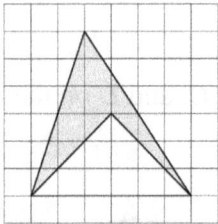

What is the area of the shaded region?

Problem 6

Betty is about to eat some of the regular polygon soup her mom made for her. She is staring at her bowl of soup, and this is what she can see:

Betty immediately noticed some of the polygons in her bowl were not regular.

What is the least number of polygons she must eat so that she can see only regular polygons?

Problem 7

How many of the fractions

$$\frac{1}{20}, \frac{2}{20}, \ldots, \frac{19}{20}, \frac{20}{20}$$

are irreducible?

Problem 8
Ms. Richards drew three similar triangles on the board and labeled the length of some of their sides.

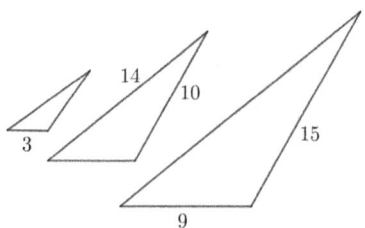

What is the perimeter of the small triangle?

Problem 9
Muriel is arranging the books in her locker. She has 2 math books and 4 literature books.

If Muriel wants all books from the same subject to be together, in how many ways can she choose how to arrange her books?

Problem 10
Connor is making a drawing with hundreds of cars. His goal is to include at least 350 cars in his drawing.

After drawing the first few cars he noticed he can draw 3 cars every 5 minutes. At this pace, how many whole minutes would he need to draw at least 350 cars?

Problem 11

Niles has a bag with 4 red marbles, 5 blue marbles and 3 yellow marbles.

Niles will grab, without looking, several marbles at once in hopes to find a blue marble. What is the smallest number of marbles Niles could grab to be completely certain that he grabbed a blue marble?

Problem 12

Paige made some popcorn for a movie watching party at her house. She made 13 bags of popcorn in total, some of them regular popcorn and the rest caramel popcorn.

If Paige had made 2 more bags of caramel popcorn she would have made two times as many bags of regular popcorn as caramel popcorn.

How many bags of regular popcorn did Paige make?

Problem 13

Paula is thinking of a three-digit number that is divisible by 4. The tens digit of the number is five more than the ones digit, and the ones digit is two times the hundreds digit.

What is the number Paula is thinking?

Problem 14
Brennan throws two fair six-sided dice and looks at the sum of the numbers he got.

The probability that the sum of the numbers is greater than 3 is $\frac{P}{Q}$ as a simplified fraction. What is $P+Q$?

Problem 15
Derek drew a trapezoid and then he drew squares on each of its sides to obtain the figure below:

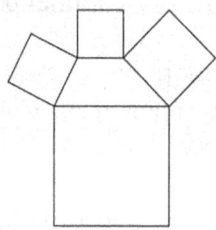

If the perimeter of the trapezoid is 12, what is the perimeter of the whole figure?

Problem 16
Sam has a bag with 100 jellybeans.

He first eats 20% of his jelly beans. Then he eats 25% of what is left in the bag. Finally he eats 30% of the jellybeans left in the bag.

How many jellybeans are still in the bag?

Problem 17
Charlie needs to set up a password for his locker. The password must be three characters long: first two consonants, and then a digit from 0 to 9.

How many different passwords could Charlie pick from?

Problem 18
Consider the following grid of black and white squares.

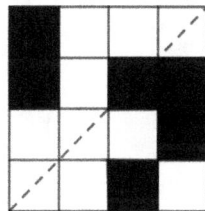

What is the least number of white squares that should be painted black so that the dotted line is a line of symmetry?

Problem 19
The students at Ms. Tyres' school went on a field trip to the park. All Preschool students rode tricycles and all Elementary school students rode bicycles.

Ms. Tyres counted 129 students and 305 wheels while making her rounds at the park.

How many Preschool students attended the field trip?

Problem 20

There is a concrete tub in Larry's patio. Measured from the outside the tub is 7 feet long, 6 feet wide, and 3 feet tall. If the sides and bottom of the tub are 1 feet thick, how many cubic feet of concrete were needed to build the tub?

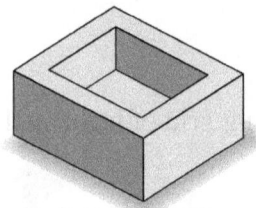

1.7 ZIML April 2019 Division E

Below are the 20 Problems from the Division E ZIML Competition held in April 2019.
The answer key is available on p.176 in the Appendix.
Full solutions to these questions are available starting on p.139.

Problem 1
A group of 5 ants can build a bridge in 3 days. How many ants are needed to build a bridge in 1 day?

Problem 2
A square has twice the area of a rectangle that has one side of length 4 and a perimeter of 12.

What is the side length of the square?

Problem 3
Elise broke her piggy bank and found she has $25.35 in quarters and dimes. If she has exactly 21 dimes, how many quarters does she have?

Problem 4
In the following diagram made of squares, the smallest squares each have area 1.

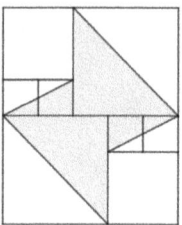

What is the area of the shaded region?

Problem 5
At the Lagunitas soccer school, 64% of the kids are elementary school students, and the rest are middle school students. If there are 208 elementary school students, how many middle school students are there?

Problem 6
Erik randomly chooses a number from $10, 11, 12, \ldots, 30$. The probability that he chooses a number that is a multiple of 3 is $\frac{P}{Q}$ as a simplified fraction. What is $Q - P$?

Problem 7
The sum of the squares of two numbers is 89. What is the smaller of the two numbers?

Problem 8
Three congruent large rectangles and six congruent small rectangles are arranged to form a larger rectangle, as pictured in the diagram below.

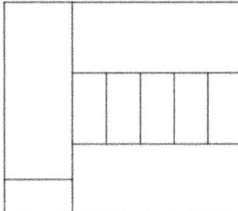

If each of the large rectangles has area 25, what is the area of the larger rectangle?

Problem 9
Mackenzie had a bag with some apples. All together the bag full of apples had a weight of 12 pounds. After she gave away half of the apples her bag of apples had a weight of 7 pounds. What is the weight of the empty bag, in pounds?

Problem 10
A number between 200 and 250 is such that (i) it leaves no remainder when divided by 6, (ii) it leaves remainder 2 when divided by 5. What is the number?

Problem 11
A quadrilateral is inscribed in a rectangle, as pictured in the diagram below.

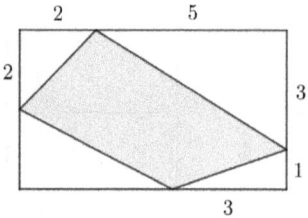

What is the area of the shaded region?

Problem 12
Prue baked a pie and sliced it into 7 slices. Three of the slices were twice as big as the rest, which were all the same size. If Prue measured the angle in one of the big slices, how many degrees would that angle be?

Problem 13
Moira needs to buy some flower bouquets. All of the bouquets are the same price. If she buys 5 of bouquets she will have $17 left over. If she buys 8 of them she will be $22 short. How much does each bouquet cost? Give your answer in dollars rounded to the nearest cent.

Problem 14

A sequence of numbers starts with

$$3, -6, -12, 24, -48, -96, \ldots$$

Continuing this pattern, what is the 8th term of the sequence?

Problem 15

Sally had two pieces of chocolate. One was 15 centimeters long and the other one was 9 centimeters long.

She first split each piece of chocolate in three equal sized pieces. Then, she split any pieces that were longer than 4 centimeters in half.

How many pieces of chocolate does Sally have now?

Problem 16

What is the largest three-digit number that has no repeated digits and is a multiple of 3?

Problem 17

Pierre painted a figure on a square grid, as pictured in the diagram below.

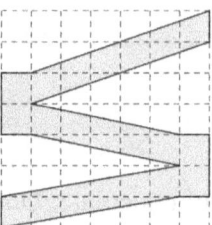

If the grid is made out of unit squares, what is the area of Pierre's figure?

Problem 18

When the stocks of Carbonite Soda were $24.45 a piece, Rita bought $4890 worth of stocks.

Now her stocks are worth $6250. What is the current price of a single stock in dollars? Round your answer to the nearest cent.

Problem 19
What is the surface area, in square inches, of the triangular prism in the diagram below?

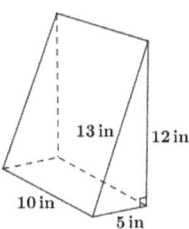

Problem 20
Rebbecca wrote all the numbers from 200 to 400 on a piece of paper. How many times did she write the digit 2?

1.8 ZIML May 2019 Division E

Below are the 20 Problems from the Division E ZIML Competition held in May 2019.
The answer key is available on p.177 in the Appendix.
Full solutions to these questions are available starting on p.146.

Problem 1
In the following diagram the smallest square has perimeter 4 and the second smallest square has perimeter 8.

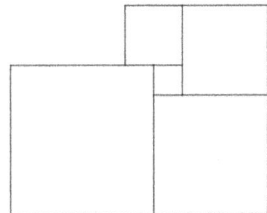

What is the perimeter of the whole figure?

Problem 2
At the food court the cooks have noticed that the number of people that eat mashed potatoes and the number of people that eat mac and cheese are in ratio 3 : 5. Given that a person must choose either mashed potatoes or mac and cheese with their meal and they need to feed 224 people, how many servings of mashed potatoes should they prepare?

Problem 3
Gloria has been keeping track of how much water she drinks for the past few days and made a table with her numbers:

Monday	Tuesday	Wednesday	Thursday	Friday
10	9	11	7	

Her goal is to drink, on average, 9 or more glasses of water per day. How many glasses of water does Gloria need to drink on Friday to achieve her goal?

Problem 4
Bob and Dylan start running from the same place in the same direction, each at a constant speed. 5 seconds after they start running Bob is 15 meters ahead of Dylan. If Dylan runs at 15 meters per second, what is Bob's speed? Give your answer in meters per second rounded to the nearest tenth.

Problem 5
Dolly baked 2-inch mini pizzas as appetizers for a cocktail party. She was hungry so she ate 2 of them right away.

Her guests ate half of the mini pizzas within the first hour, and two thirds of the remaining mini pizzas within the next hour. There were then 8 mini pizzas left.

How many mini pizzas did Dolly bake?

Problem 6

Annabelle wants to fence around a rectangular yard with length 50 yards and width 30 yards. She also wants to put some fencing to divide her yard into two rectangles with equal area.

If Anabelle wants to use the least amount of fence possible, how many yards of fence should buy she to achieve her goal?

Problem 7

There are 9 red cubes, 5 red balls, 4 green cubes, and 6 green balls in a bag. Sally grabs one object from the bag at random.

The probability that she grabs a cube or a red object is $P\%$. What is P? Round your answer to the nearest tenth.

Problem 8

In her art class, Marty was instructed to paint a landscape that included: the Sun, three birds, and two fruit trees. The Sun can be either yellow or orange (depending if the landscape is set at noon or at sunset). The birds can be blue, yellow, or white, but all have to be the same color. The fruit trees could be either red (for apple trees) or peach (for peach trees), and Marty may choose to make them different.

According to these instructions, how many different choices does Marty have for the above colors when drawing his landscape?

Problem 9

Katya cut four identical rectangles and glued their ends together to produce the figure in the diagram below.

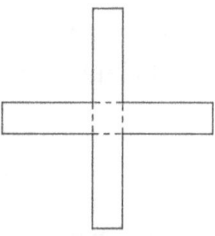

If each rectangle has length 8 and width 2, what is the area of the resulting figure?

Problem 10

A four-digit number is such that (i) the sum of its digits is 27 and (ii) the two-digit number obtained by looking at its first two digits is twice the two-digit number obtained by looking at its last two digits.

If the first digit of this four-digit number is 9, what is the number?

Problem 11
Derek can write a 1000-word essay for his English class in 30 minutes. He loves History, so he usually spends 20% less time writing History essays than English essays.

If Derek needs to write a 2000-word essay for his History class, how much time would he need to complete his assignment? Give your answer in minutes rounded to the nearest whole minute.

Problem 12
In the following diagram all line segments intersect at 90° angles, and the smallest line segments have length 2.

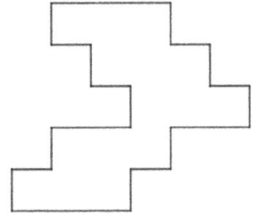

What is the area of the figure?

Problem 13

Each time Esteban goes to Taco Bell he gets three packets of Fire sauce. He does not always use all of his sauce packets, so he saves the leftovers in a small drawer.

He just noticed that his drawer is almost full of sauce packets and wonders how many he has. He estimates that 50% of the time he only uses 1 sauce packet, 25% of the time he uses 2 sauce packets, and he uses all three of them the rest of the time.

If he visited Taco Bell 48 times since he started saving his extra sauce packets, how many sauce packets are currently in the drawer?

Problem 14

In the following diagram $\triangle ABC$ is isosceles.

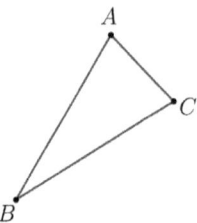

If $\angle A = 72°$, what is the angle measure of $\angle B$? Give your answer in degrees rounded to the nearest tenth.

Problem 15

Astrid wants to use construction paper to make a house like the one in the diagram below.

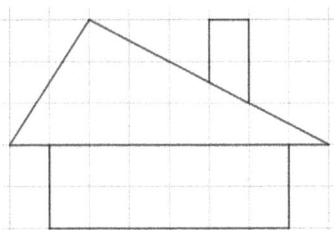

If Astrid wants the base of her house to be a rectangle with length 12 inches and width 4 inches, what is the total area of the construction paper she will use to build her house? Give your answer in square inches rounded to the nearest whole number.

Problem 16

Rita's mom just told her that there are 36 popsicles in the freezer. Rita went to the freezer to check and was confused since she counted 52 popsicle sticks. When Rita asked her mom, she told her that some of the popsicles were "double popsicles", so they'd have two sticks. (Each "double popsicles" is still counted as one popsicle.)

How many "double popsicles" are there in Rita's freezer?

Problem 17
Ron arranged several regular pentagons of side length 3 as pictured in the diagram below.

What is the perimeter of Ron's figure?

Problem 18
Sol works in the produce department at the grocery store. She needs to make a stack of oranges from a box that contains 74 oranges. She starts by making a row of 12 oranges. Then she places a second row of oranges on top of that first row, so that one orange rests on two adjacent oranges from the first row. As she continues making rows, she notices that each time she uses less oranges per row.

If she keeps going in this manner, placing as many oranges per row as possible, how many rows of oranges will her stack have once she is done placing all 74 oranges in it?

1.8 ZIML May 2019 Division E

Problem 19

Landy is studying white rabbits and brown rabbits at the park. She noticed that white rabbits always make 30-inch jumps and brown rabbits always make 40-inch jumps.

A brown rabbit starts jumping in a straight line and jumps a total of 1000 inches. A little while later, Landy notices that a white rabbit starts jumping on the same line, starting from the same spot as the brown rabbit. Not counting the starting spot, how many landing spots in the 1000 inches are shared by both rabbits?

Problem 20

Tom found the mean and the median of the numbers

$$6, 4, 7, 5, \text{ and } 7,$$

but did not like that the median was larger than the mean. He wants to remove one single number from the list so that the mean is equal to the median. What number should he remove?

1.9 ZIML June 2019 Division E

Below are the 20 Problems from the Division E ZIML Competition held in June 2019.
The answer key is available on p.178 in the Appendix.
Full solutions to these questions are available starting on p.154.

Problem 1
A rectangle with perimeter 24 is twice as long as it is wide. What is the area of this rectangle?

Problem 2
A truck moves at a constant speed of 60 miles per hour for 20 minutes, and then at a constant speed of 50 miles per hour for 30 minutes. How many miles did the truck travel during this time? Give your answer in miles rounded to the nearest mile.

Problem 3
In the following diagram the squares have side length 1, 2, 3, and 4.

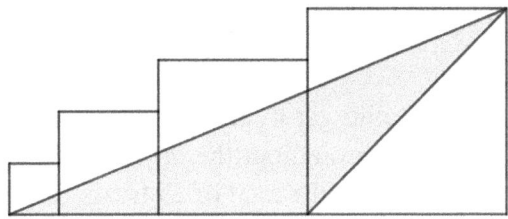

What is the area of the shaded region?

Problem 4
Bunny, the rabbit, had a big stash of carrots. He ate two-thirds of his carrots, gave away 20 carrots to his friend Loonie, and then ate half of his remaining carrots.

If he has now 23 carrots, how many carrots did Bunny originally have?

Problem 5
In the following diagram the three small circles have the same radius.

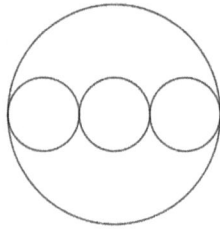

If the area of one of the small circles is $4 \times \pi$, the area of the large circle is $K \times \pi$ for some integer K. What is K?

Problem 6
Dogs Petra and Rollie get treats at the end of each day if they were well behaved throughout the day. During the past month Petra and Rollie received a total of 29 treats. If Petra received 5 more treats than Rollie, how many treats did Petra receive?

Problem 7
Raquel is making a diagram of a rocket like the one pictured below.

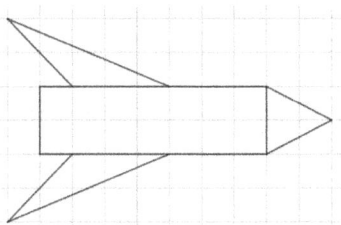

She will use four pieces of paper of different colors: three triangles, and one rectangle.

In the diagram the square grid is made out of unit squares. What is the total area of the paper Raquel used?

Problem 8
At the beginning of the school year Clara had the same number of red pencils and blue pencils. After a few months she had lost $\frac{2}{5}$ of her red pencils and $\frac{2}{3}$ of her blue pencils. She has now $\frac{P}{Q}$ of her pencils left. If the fraction $\frac{P}{Q}$ is in lowest terms, what is $Q - P$?

Problem 9
At Make-A-Burger guests can personalize their hamburgers by choosing the type of bread, the type of meat, and what veggies they want. There are 3 different types of bread, 4 types of meat, and guests can choose if they want lettuce, onions, tomato and pickles.

In how many different ways can a guest order a burger?

Problem 10
Adrienne draw three similar triangles, each bigger than the previous one, by making the sides two times larger than the previous triangle. Her first triangle is pictured below.

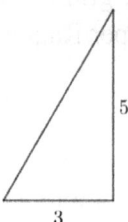

What is the area of her third triangle?

Problem 11
How many of the numbers $1, 2, 3, \ldots, 20$, have more than 2 factors?

Problem 12

Esteban wants to build a kite. He has two sticks of lengths 3 feet and 5 feet, thread, newspaper, and tape.

He'll start by making a cross with the two sticks, joining them with some thread, as in the diagram below.

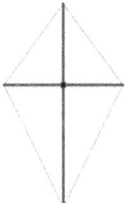

Then he'll join the ends of the sticks with thread to make the perimeter of the kite. Finally, he will tape newspaper to the kite's "skeleton".

What is the area of the newspaper that Esteban will use to make his kite? Give your answer in square feet rounded to the nearest tenth.

Problem 13
Toby is an aspiring writer. Each day he brings some blank paper with him in case he comes up with ideas to write. At the beginning of each day he makes sure he has enough paper for the day. To decide how much paper to bring, he looks at the median of the number of pieces of paper he's used over the past seven days and brings two additional pieces of paper.

Over the past seven days he's used 5, 8, 6, 4, 7, 8, and 8 pieces of paper per day. How many pieces of paper will he bring with him today?

Problem 14
10 actors showed up for an audition for an upcoming play. The casting director chooses one of the actors to be the hero, and two actors to be the villains (he does not really care who is the first villain and who is the second villain).

In how many different ways can the casting director choose the actors?

Problem 15
Lauren ate breakfast at her favorite restaurant. She got a coffee for $2.80, pancakes for $4.50, and eggs with hash browns for $3.50. If tax is 7% and she tips 20% of her total before tax, how much would she pay in total? Give your answer in dollars rounded to the nearest cent.

Problem 16

For one of her art class assignments Kendra was asked to paint a small painting using Pointillism. Pointillism is a technique of painting in which small, distinct dots of color are applied in patterns to form an image.

Kendra estimates that she will need about 200,000 dots to complete her painting. If Kendra paints about 12,000 dots per hour, what percent of her painting will be complete after 5 hours? Round your answer to the nearest percent.

Problem 17

Ms. Robertson is buying supplies for her classroom. Pencils come in packs of 12 that cost $2.50 per pack, erasers come in packs of 20 that cost $2.00 per pack, and pens come in packs of 30 that cost $5.00 per pack. If she buys just enough supplies to give each of her 60 students one pencil, one eraser, and one pen, how much would she need to pay? Give an exact answer in dollars.

Problem 18
Lance had several sticks of length 1 and length 2 and used them to make a figure like the one in the diagram below.

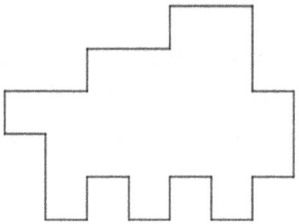

What is the perimeter of Lance's figure?

Problem 19
Ron is thinking of a number that leaves a remainder of 3 when it is divided by 7, and a remainder of 4 when it is divided by 8. If the number is between 100 and 150, what is the number?

Problem 20
Carly and Donna are playing a game. Each of them flips a coin three times and counts how many times they get heads. They win if they both get at least 2 heads.

The probability that they win the game is $\frac{P}{Q}$ as a fraction in lowest terms. What is $Q - P$?

2. ZIML Solutions

This part of the book contains the official solutions to the problems from the nine Division E ZIML Contests from the 2018-19 School Year.

Students are encouraged to discuss and share their own methods to the problems using the Discussion Forum on ziml.areteem.org.

2.1 ZIML October 2018 Division E

Below are the solutions from the Division E ZIML Competition held in October 2018.
The problems from the contest are available on p.17.

Problem 1 Solution
Since the number has three times as many hundreds as ones, it can have at most 3 ones. Since it has 2 more ones than tens, it can have 0 or 1 tens. If it had 0 tens, it would have $2 \times 0 = 0$ thousands, so it would have repeated digits. Thus, the number has 1 ten, $2 \times 1 = 2$ thousands, $1 + 2 = 3$ ones and $3 \times 3 = 9$ hundreds. Hence, the number is 2913.

Answer: 2913

Problem 2 Solution
There are triangles of 4 different sizes. We have 4 of each size, except for the biggest size, of which we have only 1. That means there are $4 \times 3 + 1 = 13$ different triangles in the diagram.

Answer: 13

Problem 3 Solution
Examining the sequence we can see every other number is obtained by multiplying the previous number in the sequence by 3 and the rest of the numbers are obtained by adding 1 to the previous number. The last number in the sequence is $66 + 1 = 67$, so the next number must be $67 \times 3 = 201$.

Answer: 201

2.1 ZIML October 2018 Division E

Problem 4 Solution

The two squares are "glued together" by one of the sides of the small square, which has side length $16 \div 4 = 4$. Thus, the perimeter of Gregory's figure is $16 + 28 - 4 \times 2 = 36$.

Answer: 36

Problem 5 Solution

We can set up a proportion to figure out how many students are there in Clementine's class. Since 3 out of every 7 students wear green swimming caps, the proportion we want to solve looks like

$$3 : 7 = 18 : \_\_.$$

Since $18 = 3 \times 6$ this means there are $7 \times 6 = 42$ students in Clementine's class.

Answer: 42

Problem 6 Solution

The difference of their ages does not vary by year, so 2 years ago Eric was still 5 years older than his brother. As Eric was twice his brother's age, Eric's brother was 5 years old and Eric was $2 \times 5 = 10$ years old. So, today Eric is $10 + 2 = 12$ years old and his brother is $5 + 2 = 7$ years old.

Answer: 7

Problem 7 Solution

Since Tommy's car can travel 1.5 meters per second, it would need $39 \div 1.5 = 26$ seconds to cross the finish line. Larry's car can travel 1.3 meters per second, so it would need $39 \div 1.3 = 30$ seconds to cross the finish line. Since Larry's car had a 2 second head start, it would arrive to the finish line $30 - 26 - 2 = 2$ seconds after Tommy's car.

Answer: 2

Problem 8 Solution

The side length of the square piece of paper is the same as the length of the base of the house, so the square piece of paper has area $10 \times 10 = 100$ square centimeters. The triangle that makes up the roof has base 10 cm and height $13 - 10 = 3$ cm, so it has area $10 \times 3 \div 2 = 15$. Thus, the whole house has area $100 + 15 = 115$ square centimeters.

Answer: 115

Problem 9 Solution

The jacket had a discount of 30%, which means Aaron just needs to pay $100\% - 30\% = 70\%$ of the tag price. That is, $49 \times 70\% = 49 \times 0.7 = \$34.30$.

Answer: 34.3

Problem 10 Solution

Since it rains every 3 days, and there are huge gusts of wind every 2 days, every 6 days both will happen on the same day (here 6 is the LCM of 2 and 3).

There are $7 \times 4 = 28$ days in 4 weeks, and $28 \div 6 = 4R4$, so there will be 4 days where it rains and there are huge gusts of wind on the same day.

Answer: 4

Problem 11 Solution

Since she can type 44 words per minute, she would need $500 \div 44 \approx 11.36$ minutes to type 500 words. So, in 12 minutes she would type over 500 words.

Answer: 12

2.1 ZIML October 2018 Division E

Problem 12 Solution
Since the yard is three times as long as it is wide, it could be split in three squares, each of area $75 \div 3 = 25$ square yards. Thus, the width of the yard is $\sqrt{25} = 5$ yards and the length of the yard is $3 \times 5 = 15$ yards. This means Manny will need $2 \times (5 + 15) = 40$ linear yards of fence.

Answer: 40

Problem 13 Solution
If she decides to pick from the green palette, she can choose one of 4 colors to paint the doors, one of $4 - 1 = 3$ colors to paint the hood, and one of $3 - 1 = 2$ colors to paint the rest of the car, that is, she can paint her car blue in $4 \times 3 \times 2 = 24$ different ways.

If she decides to go with the green palette, she has $5 \times 4 \times 3 = 60$ different choices.

Therefore, altogether she has $24 + 60 = 84$ different ways to paint her car.

Answer: 84

Problem 14 Solution
If all 11 cups had been 12-ounce cups, she would have served $11 \times 12 = 132$ ounces of juice. That is $132 - 104 = 28$ more ounces than she actually has. Every 12-ounce cup, serves $12 - 8 = 4$ more ounces than an 8-ounce cup. So there are actually $28 \div 4 = 7$ 8-ounce cups, and $11 - 7 = 4$ 12-ounce cups

Answer: 7

Problem 15 Solution

Similar triangles have proportional sides. The two shortest sides of Ms. Tammy's triangle measure 18 units and 36 units. So the sides of Candace's triangle and Ms. Tammy's triangle are in ratio $6 : 18 = 12 : 36 = 1 : 3$. Therefore the third side of Candance's triangle is $42 \div 3 = 14$ cm.

Answer: 14

Problem 16 Solution

Lola has 30 cubes. To make a cube with 2 wooden cubes per side, she would need $2 \times 2 \times 2 = 8$ wooden cubes; to make a cube with 3 wooden cubes per side, she would need $3 \times 3 \times 3 = 27$ wooden cubes; to make a cube with 4 wooden cubes per side, she would need $4 \times 4 \times 4 = 64$ wooden cubes. Thus, the biggest cube she can make will need 27 wooden cubes.

Answer: 27

Problem 17 Solution

Since the numbers are in arithmetic progression, the number in the middle of the list is the average of the smallest and the biggest numbers. That is, the number in the middle is $(19 + 107) \div 2 = 63$.

Answer: 63

Problem 18 Solution

There are a total of $5 \times 4 = 20$ possible ice cream combinations Marcie can get (5 options for the bottom scoop and $5 - 1 = 4$ options for the top scoop)

The only two ice cream flavors that do not have any chocolate are pecan nut and coffee, so there are 2 possible ice cream combinations that do not have chocolate (pecan nut on the bottom and coffee on top, or coffee on bottom and pecan nut on top).

Therefore, the probability that she does not get any chocolate ice cream is $\frac{2}{20} = 0.1 = 10\%$. Thus, $P = 10$.

Answer: 10

Problem 19 Solution

Since the maximum weight that Duncan can carry is 40 grams, that means Duncan's weight is approximately $40 \div 150 \approx 0.266$ grams. Rounded to the nearest hundredth the weight is 0.27.

Answer: 0.27

Problem 20 Solution

The cube shaped bucket can hold up to $30 \times 30 \times 30 = 27000$ cubic inches of water. The other two can hold up to $40 \times 40 \times 60 = 96000$ cubic inches of water each. Thus, the three buckets can hold $27000 + 2 \times 96000 = 219000$ cubic inches of water.

Answer: 219000

2.2 ZIML November 2018 Division E

Below are the solutions from the Division E ZIML Competition held in November 2018.
The problems from the contest are available on p.25.

Problem 1 Solution
Since the box comes with 3 layers of 15 cans, there are $3 \times 15 = 45$ cans in the box.

Thus, each can cost $72 \div 45 = 1.6$ dollars.

Answer: 1.6

Problem 2 Solution
Since he gave away 3 candies to each of his 7 friends, he have away a total of $3 \times 7 = 21$ candies. So, the bag had $21 + 5 = 26$ candies.

Answer: 26

Problem 3 Solution
Ashton will first wash three loads of clothes, which takes 30 minutes.

After the first three loads are done, he will put all three of them in the drier and load the remaining two loads in the washer. He will have to wait 45 minutes for the driers to be available again for use.

By the time the three loads of clothes are done in the drier, the last two loads he had in the washer are done. So he just needs an additional 45 minutes to dry these last two loads of clothes.

Altogether, Ashton needed $30 + 45 + 45 = 120$ minutes to wash

2.2 ZIML November 2018 Division E

and dry all of his clothes.

Answer: 120

Problem 4 Solution

The perimeter of Ivy's pinwheel is made of four segments of length 13 and four segments whose length is the difference between the length of the two shorter sides of the triangles.

Thus, the perimeter of the pinwheel is

$$4 \times 13 + 4 \times (12-5) = 4 \times 20 = 80$$

inches.

Answer: 80

Problem 5 Solution

Since Valerie can write 500 words in 25 minutes, in 5 minutes she can write $500 \div 5 = 100$ words.

Note $60 \div 5 = 12$, so in 60 minutes she can write $12 \times 100 = 1200$ words.

Answer: 1200

Problem 6 Solution

Recall the sum of the interior angles of a triangle is 180°, and, since both triangles share one angle, we have $\angle A + \angle B = \angle C + \angle D$.

That is, $\angle D = 75° + 55° - 45° = 85°$.

Answer: 85

Problem 7 Solution

Since Janene can finish one lap in 5 minutes and Dannie in 7 minutes, and the LCM of 5 and 7 is 35, they will both be at the finish line at the same time 35 minutes after they start running.

In 35 minutes Janene can run $35 \div 5 = 7$ laps around the track, and Dannie can run $35 \div 7 = 5$ laps around the track.

Therefore they run $7 + 5 = 12$ laps combined.

Answer: 12

Problem 8 Solution

The number of gallons of blue and green paint he will need are in ratio $2 : 3$, so for every $2 + 3 = 5$ gallons of paint, 2 will be blue and 3 will be green.

This means he needs to buy $8 \div 5 \times 2 = 3.2$ gallons of blue paint and $8 \div 5 \times 3 = 4.8$ gallons of green paint.

Answer: 4.8

Problem 9 Solution

The shortest side of her courtyard is 9 ft. Since she wants this side to be 10 cm long in her diorama, every 9 feet in the real courtyard will be 10 cm in her diorama.

The perimeter of her courtyard is $9 + 12 + 18 + 15 = 54$ feet, so the perimeter of the courtyard in the diorama is $54 \div 9 \times 10 = 60$ centimeters.

Answer: 60

2.2 ZIML November 2018 Division E

Problem 10 Solution
The largest 4-digit number Patricia can make is 9732, and the smallest number she can make is 1023.

Thus, the difference between the largest and smallest numbers Patricia can make is $9732 - 1023 = 8709$.

Answer: 8709

Problem 11 Solution
The new exchange rate is equal to $100 + 3.2 = 103.2\%$ of the Monday exchange rate, that is

$$20 \times 103.2\% = 20 \times 1.032 = 20.64$$

MXN, which is still 20.64 MXN rounded to the nearest cent.

Answer: 20.64

Problem 12 Solution
Since the smaller square is divided into three equal parts by the lines from the other two squares, we can split the whole figure into smaller regions whose areas are easier to find:

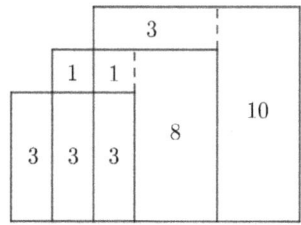

Thus, the whole figure has area $3 + 3 + 3 + 1 + 1 + 8 + 3 + 10 = 32$.

Answer: 32

Problem 13 Solution

Out of the 20 cards there are 5 blue cards with an even number and 3 black cards with a number that is a multiple of 3.

Thus, the probability is $\frac{8}{20} = \frac{2}{5}$. Therefore $Q - P = 5 - 2 = 3$.

Answer: 3

Problem 14 Solution

Since the area of the square portion is 16 square yards, the square has a side length of 4 yards.

Thus, the small rectangle has length 4 yards and width 2 yards, and the big rectangles have length $4 + 2 = 6$ yards and width 4 yards.

Marissa will need 4 pieces of fence of length 6 yards, 1 piece of fence of length $6 + 4 = 10$ yards, 2 pieces of fence of length $3 \times 4 = 12$ yards, and 2 pieces of fence of length 4 yards.

Altogether, Marissa will need

$$4 \times 6 + 1 \times 10 + 2 \times 12 + 2 \times 4 = 66$$

yards of fence.

Answer: 66

2.2 ZIML November 2018 Division E

Problem 15 Solution

Recall the average of the grades is equal to the sum of all grades divided by the number of grades.

Thus, the sum of all grades, except Tamika's, is $81 \times 16 = 1296$, and the sum of all grades is $82 \times 17 = 1394$.

Therefore, Tamika's grade was $1394 - 1296 = 98$ points.

Answer: 98

Problem 16 Solution

After pouring 15 buckets of water into the tank, there are $5 \times 15 = 75$ gallons of water in the tank.

Since 1 gallon of water equals 231 cubic inches, there are $75 \times 231 = 17325$ cubic inches of water in the tank.

We can think of the water inside the tank as a rectangular prism itself, with the same base as the rectangular prism that makes the tank. The volume of the "water prism" is 17325 cubic inches, and also $20 \times 10 \times h$, where h is its height.

Therefore, the height of the prism is

$$17325 \div 200 = 86.625$$

inches. Rounded to the nearest inch this is 87.

Answer: 87

Problem 17 Solution

Since there are 63360 inches in 1 mile, and 60 minutes in 1 hour, the average speed of a garden snail is

$$0.03 \, \frac{\text{mi}}{\text{h}} \times \frac{63360 \, \text{in}}{1 \, \text{mi}} \times \frac{1 \, \text{h}}{60 \, \text{min}}$$
$$= 0.03 \times 1056 \approx 31.7$$

which is the snail's speed in inches per minute.

Answer: 31.7

Problem 18 Solution

If Deena decides to go with the lunch special, she has 2 choices for the first course, 3 choices for the entree and 2 choices for the dessert, so she can order in $2 \times 3 \times 2 = 12$ different ways.

If she orders from the regular menu, she has 4 choices for soup, 6 choices for an entree, and 4 desserts, so she can order in $4 \times 6 \times 4 = 96$ different ways.

Altogether, Deena can order lunch in $12 + 96 = 108$ different ways.

Answer: 108

Problem 19 Solution

If Clementine had bought all 15 bags of 150 candies, she would have had in total $15 \times 150 = 2250$ candies, $2250 - 1950 = 300$ more than she has in her bowl.

A bag of 150 candies has $150 - 100 = 50$ more candies than a bag with 100 candies.

So, she bought $300 \div 50 = 6$ bags of 100 candies.

Answer: 6

Problem 20 Solution

An angle of 60° represents $\frac{1}{6}$ of a circle. So Brian's pattern will be "copied" by the mirrors 6 times producing the new figure

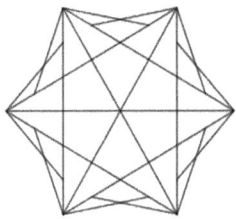

which has 6 lines of symmetry.

Answer: 6

2.3 ZIML December 2018 Division E

Below are the solutions from the Division E ZIML Competition held in December 2018.
The problems from the contest are available on p.35.

Problem 1 Solution

We can group together all the numbers that are multiplying and all the numbers that are dividing to obtain

$$\frac{10 \times 50 \times 2 \times 60}{16 \times 15}$$

which then we can simplify by looking at numbers on the numerator and denominator that have common factors (for example, 60 and 15 have a common factor of 15, so they cancel and leave a factor of 4 on top)

$$\frac{10 \times 50 \times 2 \times 60}{16 \times 15} = \frac{10 \times 50 \times 2 \times 4}{16}$$
$$= \frac{10 \times 50 \times 2}{4}$$
$$= 5 \times 50$$

so the expression is equal to 250.

Answer: 250

Problem 2 Solution

The rectangular prism is 5 by 4 by 3, so there are

$$5 \times 4 \times 3 = 60$$

total boxes of chocolate. As each box is 20 pounds, there are $60 \times 20 = 1200$ pounds of chocolate in total.

Answer: 1200

Problem 3 Solution

Using the approximation 1 mi = 1600 m, and the fact that there are $60 \times 60 = 3600$ seconds in one hour we have that

$$45\,\frac{\text{mi}}{\text{h}} \times \frac{1600\,\text{m}}{1\,\text{mi}} \times \frac{1\,\text{h}}{3600\,\text{s}} = \frac{45 \times 1600}{3600}\,\frac{\text{m}}{\text{s}} = 20\,\frac{\text{m}}{\text{s}}$$

so a hummingbird can fly up to 20 meters per second.

Answer: 20

Problem 4 Solution

Brant splits his dough in half each time, that means each time he splits his dough he gets twice as many pieces as he had before. In total, Brant would have $2 \times 2 \times 2 \times 2 = 16$ smaller pieces of dough.

Similarly, Byron obtains three times as many pieces of dough each time. In total, Byron would have $3 \times 3 \times 3 = 27$ smaller pieces of dough.

Altogether they have $16 + 27 = 43$ smaller pieces of dough to make their mini pizza.

Answer: 43

Problem 5 Solution

Altogether, there are 9 triangles of side length 1, 3 triangles of side length 2, and one triangle of side length 3.

Of these, there is 1 triangle of side length 1, 2 triangles of side length 2, and 1 triangle of side length 3 that contain the shaded triangle.

So, there are $9 + 3 + 1 - 1 - 2 - 1 = 9$ triangles that do not contain the shaded triangle.

Answer: 9

Problem 6 Solution

Dolores needs to buy the least number of packs so that the number of jars and the number of lids is a multiple of both 8 and 20.

The smallest number that is a multiple of both 8 and 20 is 40. So, she needs to buy $40 \div 8 = 5$ packs of jars and $40 \div 20 = 2$ packs of lids.

Answer: 2

Problem 7 Solution

First note that the percentage of juice in one service is the same as the percentage of juice in 3 servings.

In 3 servings there is 2 cups of orange juice out of (ignoring the hot sauce) $2 + 1 + 1 = 4$ total cups. This is

$$\frac{2}{4} = \frac{1}{2} = 0.5 = 50\%$$

so $P = 50$.

Answer: 50

Problem 8 Solution

Looking at the numbers in pairs, we notice (i) every second number is one more than the previous, and (ii) that,

$$1+2=3, 3+4=7, 7+8=15, 15+16=31, \ldots.$$

Therefore, the next number is $31 + 32 = 63$.

Answer: 63

Problem 9 Solution

Since Jonathan tested the die 100 times, we immediately see the probability of rolling a 1 is 15%, rolling a 3 is 16%, and rolling a

2.3 ZIML December 2018 Division E

5 is 19%. Therefore the probability Jonathan gets an odd number is
$$15\% + 16\% + 19\% = 50\%$$
so $P = 50$.

Answer: 50

Problem 10 Solution
We know the two triangles are similar. Therefore, as $10 \div 2 = 5$, the other two sides of the smaller triangle are
$$24 \div 2 = 12 \text{ and } 26 \div 2 = 13.$$
Therefore the final figure has sides of 26, $24 - 5 = 19$, 13, and $10 + 12 = 22$. Therefore the perimeter is $26 + 19 + 13 + 22 = 80$.

Answer: 80

Problem 11 Solution
If Lindsey had 12 more pack of Hot sauce, she would have $116 + 12 = 128$ packs of sauce in total, and she would have the same number of packs of Fire sauce and Hot sauce.

This means she has $128 \div 2 = 64$ packs of Fire sauce.

Answer: 64

Problem 12 Solution
We know the width of the rectangle is 12. As 3 small squares and 2 medium squares made up this side length, we see each small square has a side length of $12 \div 3 = 4$ and each medium square has a side length of $12 \div 2 = 6$.

Then note that the length of the rectangle is made up of 3 small squares and 1 medium square. Hence the length is
$$3 \times 4 + 6 = 12 + 6 = 18.$$

Copyright © ARETEEM INSTITUTE. All rights reserved.

Multiplying, the area is $12 \times 18 = 216$.

Answer: 216

Problem 13 Solution
Consider the diagram below, where Sally starts on the bottom edge.

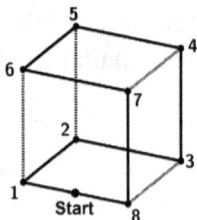

If Sally visits the vertices in the order listed, she visits all the shaded edges, a total of 8. There are 8 total vertices, and as each new edge she visits leads to a new vertex, the 8 edges is the maximum possible.

Answer: 8

Problem 14 Solution
Each cupcake has a diameter of 5 cm, so it has a circumference of
$$\pi \times d = \pi \times 5 \approx \frac{22}{7} \times 5 = \frac{110}{7}.$$
Since 3 m is the same as 300 cm, this means Cristy has enough frosting for
$$300 \div \frac{110}{7} = 300 \times \frac{7}{110} = \frac{210}{11}$$
cupcakes. As $210 \div 11 = 19$ with remainder 1, she has enough for 19 cupcakes.

Answer: 19

2.3 ZIML December 2018 Division E 113

Problem 15 Solution

Since Paul can drink $2\frac{1}{4} = 2.25$ gallons of milk in 25 minutes, he can drink $2.25 \div 25 = 0.09$ gallons of milk per minute.

One quart is equal to 0.25 gallons, so at this rate Paul would need $0.25 \div 0.09 = 2.\overline{7} \approx 3$ minutes to drink one quart of milk.

Answer: 3

Problem 16 Solution

Every two jumps Ella gets $2 - 1 = 1$ meter closer to her favorite tree.

After $2 \times 13 = 26$ jumps she will land 13 meters away from her starting point, that is, $15 - 13 = 2$ meters away from the tree.

With one more 2 meter jump Ella would reach the tree, so she needs $26 + 1 = 27$ jumps to reach her favorite tree in the park.

Answer: 27

Problem 17 Solution

The numbers 44 and 51 are counted by the same person, so the number of people is a factor of $51 - 44 = 7$. Because 7 is prime, there must be 7 total people (as Penelope is not alone).

Therefore Penelope counts the numbers

$$1, 8, 15, 22, 29, \ldots$$

where all of these numbers are 1 more than a multiple of 7. $140 = 7 \times 20$, so Penelope counts 141. The next number she would count (148) is too large, so 141 is the last number she counts.

Answer: 141

Copyright © ARETEEM INSTITUTE. All rights reserved.

Problem 18 Solution

Counting by rows, there are

$$5+7+7+5=24$$

total triangles in the hexagon.

The equilateral triangles of area 1 can only be rearranged to form larger equilateral triangles. Looking at patterns, we see the larger equilateral triangles can have area

$$1^2 = 1, 2^2 = 4, 3^2 = 9, 4^2 = 16, 5^2 = 25,\ldots.$$

(All these are perfect squares.) Therefore the largest possible triangle has area 16.

Answer: 16

Problem 19 Solution

We know that $99 = 9 \times 11$. Therefore, the smallest number that has 3 digits and leaves a remainder of 7 when divided by 11 is $99 + 7 = 106$. We can find more of these numbers by adding 11 to 106, so the next few numbers that leave a remainder of 7 when divided by 11 are

$$117, 128, 139, 150, 161, 172, \ldots$$

Because we want the number to leave a remainder of 4 when it is divided by 5, the number must end in either 4 or 9. By looking at our list of numbers, we see the smallest of them that ends in 4 or 9 is 139, so this is the number we are looking for.

Answer: 139

Problem 20 Solution

All numbers are divisible by 1, so all numbers that have tens digit 1 are "funny". We have 10 of those:

$$110, 111, \ldots, 119.$$

For the numbers with tens digit 2, the even numbers work. These are
$$110, 112, 114, 116, 118,$$
a total of 5. Continuing we can find the numbers:

Tens Digit	Numbers	Total
3	132, 135, 138	3
4	140, 144, 148	3
5	150, 155	2

Therefore in total there are
$$10 + 5 + 3 + 3 + 2 = 23$$
total "funny" numbers from 100 to 160.

Answer: 23

2.4 ZIML January 2019 Division E

Below are the solutions from the Division E ZIML Competition held in January 2019.
The problems from the contest are available on p.43.

Problem 1 Solution
Recall that the area of a triangle is given by $A = \dfrac{b \times h}{2}$, where b is the length of the base of the triangle and h is the height of the triangle. Thus, $90 \times 2 = 180$ is equal to the product of the base and the height of the triangle. Note that $180 = 6 \times 30$, and $30 = 6 \times 5$, so the height of the triangle is 30 an the base is 6.

Answer: 6

Problem 2 Solution
The smallest 3-digit number that can be formed with the digits 0, 2, 5 and 7 is 205.

Since there are 5 of them eating candy canes, each of them ate $205 \div 5 = 41$ candy canes.

Answer: 41

Problem 3 Solution
Since Pablo's dad can make four pots in the same time that Pablo makes three, we can put together the pots in groups of $3 + 4 = 7$ pots.

Working together they made $63 \div 7 = 9$ of this groups of pots. This means Pablo made $3 \times 9 = 27$ pots.

Answer: 27

2.4 ZIML January 2019 Division E

Problem 4 Solution
The side length of each of the small squares is 3, since $3 \times 3 = 9$.

The side length of the big square is two times the side length of the small squares, that is $2 \times 3 = 6$.

Thus, the length of the rectangles is $2 \times 6 = 12$.

Therefore, the whole figure is a rectangle with length $12 + 6 = 18$ and width $6 + 3 = 9$. Hence, it has area $9 \times 18 = 162$.

Answer: 162

Problem 5 Solution
Since Bob had twice as much money as Charles, he had $2 \times 7 = 14$ dollars. Adam had 2 more dollars than Bob, so he had $14 + 2 = 16$ dollars. This means they had $16 + 14 + 7 = 37$ dollars in total.

Answer: 37

Problem 6 Solution
The sum of the 8 numbers is

$$1 + 2 + 3 + 5 + 8 + 13 + 21 + 34 = 87.$$

Therefore the average is

$$87 \div 8 = 10\frac{7}{8}.$$

Hence 5 of the numbers in the list (up to the fifth number 8) are lower than the average, so the probability is

$$\frac{5}{8} = 0.625 = 62.5\%$$

so $P = 62.5$.

Answer: 62.5

Problem 7 Solution

To fence the perimeter of the yard Robert will need two pieces of fence of length 10 yards and two pieces of fence of length 18 yards. To divide the yard in four equal regions, Robert will need another piece of fence of length 10 yards and another piece of fence of length 18 yards.

Altogether, Robert will need $3 \times (10 + 18) = 84$ yards of fence.

Answer: 84

Problem 8 Solution

Listing the factors of 60 in pairs we have $(1,60)$, $(2,30)$, $(3,20)$, $(4,15)$, $(5,12)$, and $(6,10)$.

There are 6 pairs in total, with each pair multiplying together to get 60. Therefore multiplying out all the factors we get

$$60 \times 60 \times 60 \times 60 \times 60 \times 60.$$

Notice that we get one 0 from each 60, so there must be 6 zeros at the end if we multiply out all the factors.

Answer: 6

Problem 9 Solution

Since one of the 7 slices was twice as big as the other 6, we can pretend Larry sliced the pie into 8 equal slices, so the angle formed by each of the slices would be $360 \div 8 = 45°$. Since the bigger slice is made up of two of this smaller slices, the angle formed by the bigger slice is $2 \times 45 = 90$ degrees.

Answer: 90

Problem 10 Solution

We know Louise receives a commission of 8% of the sales she makes every week. Thus, $104 is the 8% of her sales of the week.

This means this week she sold $104 \div 0.08 = 1300$ dollars.

Answer: 1300

Problem 11 Solution
Note the largest side of the small triangle has length 6 and the largest side of the big triangle has length 12. Since the triangles are similar, this means the side lengths of the big triangle are twice as long as the side lengths of the small triangle, and thus, its perimeter is twice the perimeter of the small triangle.

The small triangle has perimeter $4 + 6 + 3 = 13$, so the big triangle has perimeter $13 \times 2 = 26$.

Answer: 26

Problem 12 Solution
Since she is the third person to open a present, there are $6 - 2 = 4$ presents to choose from. One of the presents is hers, so the probability that she picks her own present is $\frac{1}{4} = 0.25 = 25\%$.

Answer: 25

Problem 13 Solution
Drawing the midpoint on the opposite side of the square, we can divide the whole figure into 5 congruent triangles, as shown below:

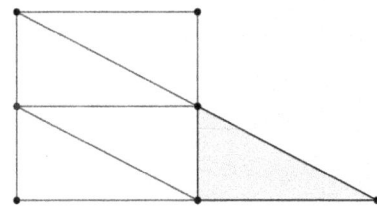

Congruent triangles all have the same area, so because the square is made up of 4 triangles, it has area $4 \times 4 = 16$.

Answer: 16

Problem 14 Solution

Lydia travels 6 miles in 45 minutes, that is, 0.75 hours. This means her speed is $6 \div 0.75 = 8$ miles per hour.

Answer: 8

Problem 15 Solution

Since the box does not have a top, Tom will need to cover two sides with dimensions 15×30 (front and back), two sides with dimensions 20×30 (left and right), and one side with dimensions 15×20 (the bottom).

The area he needs to cover is thus equal to $2 \times 15 \times 30 + 2 \times 20 \times 30 + 15 \times 20 = 2400$ square centimeters. Since he wants to cover the inside and the outside of the box, he will need in total $2400 \times 2 = 4800$ square centimeters.

Answer: 4800

Problem 16 Solution

Notice multiplying any two-digit number by 100 gives the number followed by 00. Therefore, adding the number once more gives the "doubled" number. This is the same as multiplying by 101, so $K = 101$.

Answer: 101

2.4 ZIML January 2019 Division E

Problem 17 Solution
If Trisha had jumped 1 meter every time, she would have jumped $1 \times 15 = 15$ meters in total. This means she would be $18.5 - 15 = 3.5$ meters away from the door of the school.

Every time she jumps 1.5 meters, she jumps $1.5 - 1 = 0.5$ meters more. This means she jumped 1.5 meters a total of $3.5 \div 0.5 = 7$ times.

Answer: 7

Problem 18 Solution
Since he bought 3 times as many fruit flavored packs as mint flavored packs, he bought $24 \div (3+1) = 6$ mint flavored packs and $3 \times 6 = 18$ fruit flavored packs.

Answer: 18

Problem 19 Solution
January has 31 days, so if Jenna's birthday is a perfect square, it must be one of
$$1, 4, 9, 16, \text{ or } 25.$$

If it is in the second half of the month, it must be either 16 or 25. It cannot be 25 as her birthday is not a multiple of 5.

Therefore Jenna's birthday is January 16th, so the answer is 16.

Answer: 16

Problem 20 Solution
Note the two small cubes fit perfectly across the top of the large cube. This means their side length is half that of the large cube.

This means two small cubes fit in each direction of the large cube, so $2 \times 2 \times 2 = 8$ small cubes have the same volume as the large cube.

The combined volume is 120, which must be the volume of $8+2 = 10$ small cubes. Hence each small cube has a volume of $120 \div 10 = 12$ and the large cube has a volume of $8 \times 12 = 96$.

Answer: 96

2.5 ZIML February 2019 Division E

Below are the solutions from the Division E ZIML Competition held in February 2019.
The problems from the contest are available on p.51.

Problem 1 Solution
Since Kallie has 8 trays of cookies, each with $5 \times 7 = 35$ cookies, she has $8 \times 35 = 280$ cookies in total.

As she spends an average of 6 seconds decorating each cookie, to decorate all cookies, she will need $280 \times 6 = 28 \times 60$ seconds, that is, 28 minutes.

Answer: 28

Problem 2 Solution
Regardless of the dimensions of the four rectangles we will get the same answer. Therefore we pick nice numbers for the dimensions to make the calculation easy.

Suppose the rectangle with perimeter 16 has a base of 5 and height of 3 (so its perimeter is $2(5+3) = 16$ as needed).

Therefore the rectangle with perimeter 10 also has a height of 3, so its base is $(10 - 2 \times 3) \div 2 = 2$. Note this is the base of the fourth rectangle.

Similarly the rectangle with perimeter 12 has a base of 5, so its height is $(12 - 2 \times 5) \div 2 = 1$. This is the height of the fourth rectangle.

Thus the fourth rectangle has perimeter $2 \times (2+1) = 6$.

Try using different dimensions to see you always get the same answer!

Answer: 6

Problem 3 Solution
Two of the three special edition soldiers must be on the ends. Therefore, Andy has 3 choices for which soldier is on one end and 2 choices for the other end. Hence there are $3 \times 2 = 6$ ways to decide the ends.

There are then 6 soldiers remaining, and, choosing which soldier is placed in the remaining 6 spots one by one, this can be done in

$$6 \times 5 \times 4 \times 3 \times 2 \times 1 = 720$$

ways.

In total this gives $6 \times 720 = 4320$ arrangements of the soldiers.

Answer: 4320

Problem 4 Solution
Since 3 workers take 5 hours to finish the job, assembling a dining table requires $3 \times 5 = 15$ work hours.

This means a crew of 5 workers would need to work for $15 \div 5 = 3$ hours to assemble a dining table. This is $60 \times 3 = 180$ minutes.

Answer: 180

Problem 5 Solution
Since the price tag of the TV is $800, after the 15% discount the price went down to $800 \times 0.85 = 680$ dollars.

Thus each month, Eddie will pay $680 \div 12 \approx 56.67$ dollars.

Answer: 56.67

2.5 ZIML February 2019 Division E

Problem 6 Solution

If Meredith had 2 less baseball caps, she would have $46 - 2 = 44$ baseball caps and cowboy hats in total, and exactly three times as many baseball caps as cowboy hats.

Meredith can make groups of $1 + 3 = 4$ hats, each with one cowboy hat and three baseball caps. This means she has $44 \div 4 = 11$ cowboy hats.

Answer: 11

Problem 7 Solution

Recall equilateral triangles have all 3 sides of the same length.

The first triangle has a side length of 5, so a perimeter of $3 \times 5 = 15$.

The second triangle has a side length of $2 \times 5 = 10$, so a perimeter of $3 \times 10 = 30$.

The last triangle has a side length of $5 \div 2 = 2.5$, so a perimeter of $3 \times 2.5 = 7.5$.

This gives a combined perimeter of $15 + 30 + 7.5 = 52.5$.

Answer: 52.5

Problem 8 Solution

Each of the eleven vertices of the undecagon can be connected by means of a diagonal to other 8 vertices.

If we multiply 11×8 we are counting each diagonal twice. This means an undecagon has $11 \times 8 \div 2 = 44$ diagonals.

Answer: 44

Problem 9 Solution

The ratio of small dogs to large dogs is $7:5 = 21:15$, and the ratio of large dogs to extra large dogs is $3:1 = 15:5$. Thus, combining these ratios we see the ratio of small dogs to large dogs to extra large dogs is $21:15:5$.

This means the number of dogs at the park is a multiple of $21 + 15 + 5 = 41$. The only multiple of 41 between 80 and 100 is $2 \times 41 = 82$, so there were $2 \times 15 = 30$ large dogs visiting the park this morning.

Answer: 30

Problem 10 Solution

The volume of her tank is $70 \times 40 \times 30 = 84000$ cubic centimeters, so she needs $84000 \div 1000 = 84$ liters of water.

Since the faucet pours 4 liters of water per minute, she will need $84 \div 4 = 21$ minutes to fill her tank.

Answer: 21

Problem 11 Solution

Since Lance drew only regular polygons, all the sides are the same length. Adding up the sides of a pentagon, heptagon, and nonagon we have $5 + 7 + 9 = 21$. However, 2 pairs of sides overlap (for the pentagon and heptagon and for the heptagon and nonagon). Therefore Lance's figure has $21 - 2 \times 2 = 17$ sides in total.

Each side has a length of 4, so the entire perimeter is $17 \times 4 = 68$.

Answer: 68

2.5 ZIML February 2019 Division E

Problem 12 Solution

Since her office is 26 miles away from her home, and she spent $\frac{2}{3}$ of an hour on the road last night, her average speed was

$$26 \div \frac{2}{3} = 39 \text{ miles per hour.}$$

This speed is 10 miles per hour slower than her usual average speed. Thus, her usual average speed is $39 + 10 = 49$ miles per hour.

Answer: 49

Problem 13 Solution

Dante's first triangle has an area of $\frac{1}{2} \times 6 \times 14 = 42$ square centimeters.

The second triangle has a height of 4 centimeters, so to have an area of 42 square centimeters twice its base must be 42. Therefore the length of the base should be $42 \div 2 = 21$.

Answer: 21

Problem 14 Solution

Each day of January Lindsay bought twice as much candy as a day in December, that is $2 \times 3 = 6$ pieces of candy per day. As both December and January have 31 days, Lindsay bought in total

$$3 \times 31 + 6 \times 31 = 9 \times 31 = 279$$

pieces of candy.

Answer: 279

Problem 15 Solution

The small square has an area of $2 \times 2 = 4$ square inches. However, when unfolded, this becomes 4 pieces cut out of the original

square. Thus the area of Cecilia's paper after cutting out this square is
$$10 \times 10 - 4 \times 4 = 84$$
square inches.

Answer: 21

Problem 16 Solution
There are $4 \times 4 = 16$ total ways the dice can be rolled.

We know Ariel either rolls a 3, 4, 5, or 6. Looking at each of these separately we can see which numbers for Belle will be lower.

If Ariel rolls a 3, there are 2 rolls (1 or 2) for Belle.

If Ariel rolls a 4, there are 3 rolls (1, 2, or 3) for Belle.

If Ariel rolls a 5 or a 6, all of Belle's rolls are lower. This gives $4 + 4 = 8$ more possibilities.

Therefore the probability is
$$\frac{2+3+4+4}{16} = \frac{13}{16}$$
and the answer $P + Q = 13 + 16 = 29$.

Answer: 29

Problem 17 Solution
Clue (i) tells us all the digits must be different. Therefore if the last digit is four times the first digit using clue (iii), we either have the first digit is 1 and the last digit is 4 or the first digit is 2 and the last digit is 8. Consider these as two separate cases.

In the first case our number is of the form 1_ _4. Clue (ii) says one of the remaining digits must be 2. By clue (iv) we then know the number must be 1624.

In the second case our number is of the form 2_ _8. There are no repeating digits, so using clue (iv) we either have the number 2318 or 2938.

Hence the largest number is 2938 and the smallest is 1624. The difference is $2938 - 1624 = 1314$.

Answer: 1314

Problem 18 Solution

There are no 1-digit numbers greater than 0 that use the digit 0.

All 2-digit numbers that end in 0 will have exactly one 0; there are 9 of these.

Numbers from 101 to 109 have one zero; there are 9 of these.

From 110 to 199 the only numbers with the digit 0 will be multiples of 10; there are 9 of these.

Altogether, there are $9+9+9 = 27$ from 1 to 200 that use the digit 0 exactly once.

Answer: 27

Problem 19 Solution

To get to the next number in a geometric sequence you always multiply the previous number by a common ratio. Since

$$567 \div 63 = 9 = 3^2$$

the common ratio for this geometric sequence must be 3.

Thus the second number is $63 \div 3 = 21$.

Answer: 21

Problem 20 Solution

Starting with 44, we have $44 = 42 + 2$ where 42 is a multiple of 3. Therefore using rule (ii) the 2nd number in the sequence is

$$44 \times 3 = 132.$$

132 is a multiple of 3, so using rule (i) the 3rd number is

$$132 \times 2 - 2 = 264 - 2 = 262.$$

Since 270 is a multiple of 3, so is $270 - 9 = 261$, so 262 is one more than a multiple of 3. Therefore using rule (ii) the 4th number Lance wrote is $262 + 2 = 264$.

Answer: 264

2.6 ZIML March 2019 Division E

Below are the solutions from the Division E ZIML Competition held in March 2019.
The problems from the contest are available on p.59.

Problem 1 Solution
The fraction $\frac{48}{80}$ can be simplified to $\frac{3}{5}$. We can obtain equivalent fractions to $\frac{3}{5}$ by multiplying the numerator and denominator by the same number. Multiplying the numerator and denominator by 2, 3, 4, 5... we obtain the equivalent fractions

$$\frac{3}{5}, \frac{6}{10}, \frac{9}{15}, \frac{12}{20}, \frac{25}{25}, \ldots$$

Note the fraction $\frac{12}{20}$ is such that its numerator and denominator add up to 32, so this is the fraction we were looking for. Thus, the answer is 20.

Answer: 20

Problem 2 Solution
Since $CD = 4$ and $BD = 7$, we have $BC = 7 - 4 = 3$, and, since $AC = 7$, we have $AB = 7 - 3 = 4$.

Thus, $AD = AB + BC + CD = 4 + 3 + 4 = 11$.

Answer: 11

Problem 3 Solution
If the larger number was 53 less, the sum of the numbers would be $107 - 53 = 54$, and both numbers would be the same.

This means the small number is $54 \div 2 = 27$ and the larger number is $107 - 27 = 80$.

Answer: 27

Problem 4 Solution
The ratio of pigeons to doves in the park is $3 : 5$, which is equal to $31 \times 3 : 31 \times 5 = 93 : 155$. Thus, there are 93 pigeons and 155 doves in the park, $93 + 155 = 248$ in birds altogether.

Answer: 248

Problem 5 Solution
The shaded region is equal to the area of a triangle with base 6 and height 6 minus the area of a triangle with base 6 and height 3.

Thus, the area of the shaded region is

$$\frac{6 \times 6}{2} - \frac{6 \times 3}{2} = 9.$$

Answer: 9

Problem 6 Solution
Recall regular polygons are such that all their angles are equal and all of their sides have the same size. Thus, in Betty's soup, the following are not regular polygons.

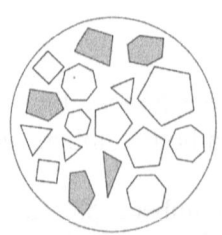

This means Betty must eat 5 non-regular polygons for her soup to have only regular polygons.

Answer: 5

Problem 7 Solution

A fraction will be irreducible if the numerator and denominator do not have any common factors (other than 1). The factors of 20 are 1, 2, 4, 5, 10, and 20.

The numbers from 1 to 20 that are not divisible by any of the factors of 20 (other than 1) are $1, 3, 7, 9, 11, 13, 17, 19$, thus 8 of the fractions are irreducible.

Answer: 8

Problem 8 Solution

Looking at the two larger triangles, we can see the ratio of their sides is $10 : 15 = 2 : 3$, so the remaining side of the large triangle is $\frac{3}{2} \times 14 = 21$.

Looking at the larger and smaller triangles, we can see the ratio of their sides is $3 : 9 = 1 : 3$, so the two remaining sides of this triangle are $15 \div 3 = 5$ and $21 \div 3 = 7$. Thus, the perimeter of this triangle is $3 + 5 + 7 = 15$.

Answer: 15

Problem 9 Solution

There are $2 \times 1 = 2$ different ways to arrange the math books together, and $4 \times 3 \times 2 \times 1 = 24$ ways to arrange the literature books together.

Muriel could also choose first to have the math books and then the literature books, or first the literature books and then the math books. So she has 2 choices for the order of the subjects.

The product rule tells us that there are $2 \times 24 \times 2 = 96$ different ways to arrange all 6 books keeping all books of the same subject together.

Answer: 96

Problem 10 Solution

For each group of 3 cars Connor will need 5 minutes to draw. We can make $\frac{350}{3} = 116\frac{2}{3}$ groups of 3 cars from the 350 cars Connor wants to draw.

So, Connor needs

$$116\frac{2}{3} \times 5 = 116 \times 5 + \frac{2}{3} \times 5$$
$$= 580 + \frac{10}{3}$$
$$= 583\frac{1}{3}$$

minutes to draw 350 cars. That is, he needs 584 whole minutes to draw at least 350 cars. (Note we round up, since 583 minutes would only be enough to draw 349 cars.)

Answer: 584

Problem 11 Solution

Let's pretend Niles grabs the marbles one by one. The worst that could happen is that he first grabs all red and yellow marbles before he grabs any blue marbles. Since there are $4 + 3 = 7$ non-blue marbles, if he grabs just one more marble he should have for sure grabbed at least one blue marble. That is, Niles needs to grab at least 8 marbles to make sure he grabbed at least one blue marble.

Answer: 8

Problem 12 Solution

Let's pretend Paige made 2 more bags of caramel popcorn. Then she made $13 + 2 = 15$ bags in total, and the ratio of regular popcorn to caramel popcorn is $2 : 1$.

Therefore, Paige made $\dfrac{2}{3} \times 15 = 10$ bags of regular popcorn.

Answer: 10

Problem 13 Solution

If the hundreds digit of Paula's number was 1, the ones digit would be 2, and the tens digit would be $5 + 2 = 7$, giving us the number 172.

If the hundreds digit of Paula's number was 2, the ones digit would be 4, and the tens digit would be $5 + 4 = 9$, giving us the number 294.

If the hundreds digit was 3, the ones digit would be 6, and the tens digit would need to be $6 + 5 = 11$, which is not a single digit number. Thus, 3 cannot be the hundreds digit. Note this would happen for any number whose hundreds digit was 3 or more, so our only candidates are 172 and 294.

From these, 172 is divisible by 4 and 294 is not. Thus, Paula's number is 172.

Answer: 172

Problem 14 Solution
There are $6 \times 6 = 36$ possible outcomes Brennan can get by throwing the two dice:

$$(1,1), (1,2), (1,3), \ldots, (6,5), (6,6).$$

From these, the only pairs that have a sum that is not greater than 3 are $(1,1)$, $(1,2)$, and $(2,1)$, so there are $36 - 3 = 33$ possible outcomes that have a sum greater than 3.

Thus, the probability that the sum of the numbers is greater than 3 is $\frac{33}{36} = \frac{11}{12}$. Therefore, $P + Q = 11 + 12 = 23$.

Answer: 23

Problem 15 Solution
Note the perimeter of the figure is equal to three times the sum of the lengths of the squares. This sum is equal to the perimeter of the trapezoid, so the perimeter of the figure is equal to three times the perimeter of the trapezoid, that is, $3 \times 12 = 36$.

Answer: 36

Problem 16 Solution
After eating 20% of his jellybeans Sam is left with $100 \times 80\% = 100 \times 0.8 = 80$ jellybeans.

Eating now 25% of the remaining jellybeans leaves Sam with $80 \times 75\% = 80 \times 0.75 = 60$ jellybeans.

Finally after eating 30% of the remaining jellybeans, there are

$60 \times 70\% = 60 \times 0.7 = 42$ jellybeans left in the bag.

Answer: 42

Problem 17 Solution
There are 21 consonants in the alphabet, so for each of the first characters of his password Charlie has 21 choices, and he has 10 choices for the digit at the end. Thus, the product rule says that Charlie could pick from $21 \times 21 \times 10 = 4410$ different passwords.

Answer: 4410

Problem 18 Solution
For the dotted line to be a line of symmetry, we need to shade the following squares:

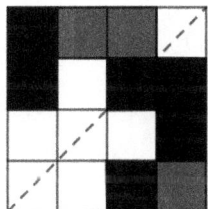

Thus, the least number of white squares that should be painted black is 3.

Answer: 3

Problem 19 Solution
Bicycles have 2 wheels and tricycles have 3 wheels.

If all students had ridden bicycles, Ms. Tyres would have counted $129 \times 2 = 258$ wheels at the park. This is $305 - 258 = 47$ less wheels than she counted.

Since a tricycle has $3 = 2 = 1$ more wheel than a bicycle, this additional 47 wheels must come from the tricycles. That is, 47 Preschool students attended the field trip.

Answer: 47

Problem 20 Solution

The volume of the tub is equal to the volume of a prism with length 7 feet, width 6 feet, and height 3 feet, minus the volume of a prism with length $7 - 2 = 5$ feet, width $6 - 2 = 4$ feet and height $3 - 1 = 2$ feet.

Thus, $7 \times 6 \times 3 - 5 \times 4 \times 2 = 86$ cubic feet of concrete were needed to build the tub.

Answer: 86

2.7 ZIML April 2019 Division E

Below are the solutions from the Division E ZIML Competition held in April 2019.
The problems from the contest are available on p.67.

Problem 1 Solution
Since we want the ants to build the bridge 3 times faster, we need to have a group of ants that is 3 times larger. Thus, $5 \times 3 = 15$ ants can build a bridge in 1 day.

Answer: 15

Problem 2 Solution
Since the rectangle has perimeter 12 and two of its sides have length 4, the other two sides have length

$$(12 - 2 \times 4) \div 2 = 2.$$

Thus, the rectangle has area 8, and the square has area $2 \times 8 = 16$. Therefore, as $4 \times 4 = 16$, the side length of the square is 4.

Answer: 4

Problem 3 Solution
All together Elise has $21 \times 0.10 = 2.10$ dollars in dimes, so she has $25.35 - 2.10 = 23.25$ dollars in quarters. Each quarter is 0.25 dollars, so she has $23.25 \div 0.25 = 93$ quarters.

Answer: 93

Problem 4 Solution
Since the smallest squares have area 1, they also have side length 1. This tells us that the other squares have side lengths of $1 + 1 = 2$ and $2 + 1 = 3$.

The shaded region has area equal to the area of one big square and two smaller squares, so it has area $3 \times 3 + 2 \times 1 = 11$.

Answer: 11

Problem 5 Solution

Since 64% of the kids are elementary school students, $100\% - 64\% = 36\%$ of the students are middle school students.

Seeing that there are 208 elementary school students enrolled at the soccer school, there are a total of $208 \div 64\% = 208 \div 0.64 = 325$ students enrolled. Therefore, there are $325 \times 36\% = 325 \times 0.36 = 117$ middle school students enrolled at the soccer school.

Answer: 117

Problem 6 Solution

Among the numbers to choose from, the multiples of 3 are $12, 15, 18, 21, 24, 27, 30$, 7 multiples of 3 in total.

Since there are a total of $30 - 10 + 1 = 21$ numbers to choose from, the probability of choosing a multiple of 3 is

$$\frac{7}{21} = \frac{1}{3}.$$

Therefore $Q - P = 3 - 1 = 2$.

Answer: 2

Problem 7 Solution

The sum of the two numbers is an odd number, so one of the numbers must be even and the other one odd.

The odd square numbers less than 89 are $1^2 = 1$, $3^2 = 9$, $5^2 = 25$, $7^2 = 49$, and $9^2 = 81$. The even square numbers less than 89 are $2^2 = 4$, $4^2 = 16$, $6^2 = 36$, and $8^2 = 64$.

Looking at the ones digits of the squares we can see the only pairs of numbers that could work are 4 and 25, or 64 and 25. $25 + 64 = 89$, so the numbers are 5 and 8. The smaller of the two numbers is 5.

Answer: 5

Problem 8 Solution
Five of the small rectangles have the same area as one of the large rectangles. Thus, the area of each of the small rectangles is $25 \div 5 = 5$.

The area of the larger rectangle is equal to 4 times the area of a large rectangle plus the area of one of the small rectangles, that is, $4 \times 25 + 5 = 105$.

Answer: 105

Problem 9 Solution
After giving away half of her apples, the weight of her bag changed from 12 to 7 pounds, so half of her apples must weigh $12 - 7 = 5$ pounds.

Thus, the weight of all the apples is $5 \times 2 = 10$ pounds, and the weight of the empty bag is $12 - 10 = 2$ pounds.

Answer: 2

Problem 10 Solution
The multiples of 6 between 200 and 250 are 204, 210, 216, 222, 228, 234, 240, and 246.

To have a remainder of 2 when divided by 5, the number must end in 2 or 7. The only such number from the list above is 222, so that is the number.

Answer: 222

Problem 11 Solution

The rectangle has width $3+1=4$ and length $2+5=7$ so it has area $4 \times 7 = 28$. Further, the bottom left triangle has base $7-3=4$ and height $4-2=2$.

The shaded region has area equal to the area of the rectangle minus the area of the four triangles in the corners. The combined area of the four triangles is

$$\frac{2 \times 2}{2} + \frac{5 \times 3}{2} + \frac{3 \times 1}{2} + \frac{2 \times 4}{2} = 15,$$

so the shaded region has area $28 - 15 = 13$.

Answer: 13

Problem 12 Solution

Since three of the slices are twice as big as the rest, we can pretend each of the big slices is two small slices. Thus, Prue would have sliced her pie into $7+3=10$ equal sized slices, and each of this slices would have an angle of $360 \div 10 = 36$ degrees. Since a big slice is twice as big as a small slice, the angle in a big slice is also twice as big as the angle in a small slice.

Therefore, each of the big slices of pie forms an angle of $36 \times 2 = 72$ degrees.

Answer: 72

Problem 13 Solution

Since Moira has $17 more than what she needs to buy 5 bouquets, and $22 less than what she needs to buy 8 bouquets, to buy $8-5=3$ bouquets, she would need $17+22=39$ dollars. Thus, each bouquet costs $39 \div 3 = 13$ dollars.

Answer: 13

2.7 ZIML April 2019 Division E

Problem 14 Solution

If we look at the first few numbers in the sequence without looking at their signs, we can see they double each time: $6 = 3 \times 2$, $12 = 6 \times 2$, $24 = 12 \times 2$, etc. This means the seventh number should be $96 \times 2 = 192$, and the eight number $192 \times 2 = 384$.

The signs of the numbers in the sequence follow the pattern $+, -, -, +, -, -, \ldots$, so the eight number should have a $-$. Thus, the eight term of the sequence is -384.

Answer: -384

Problem 15 Solution

After splitting the chocolate piece that was 15 centimeters long, she obtained three pieces of length $15 \div 3 = 5$ centimeters. After splitting the chocolate piece that was 9 centimeters long, she obtained three pieces of length 3 centimeters.

This means she split each of the three 5 centimeter pieces in two, obtaining $3 \times 2 = 6$ pieces each of length 2.5 centimeters.

Thus, altogether Sally ended up with $3 + 6 = 9$ pieces of chocolate.

Answer: 9

Problem 16 Solution

The largest three-digit number that is a multiple of 3 is 999, which has repeated digits. We can count backwards from there to find the next few multiples of 3:

$$996, 993, 990, 987, \ldots$$

The first number to appear on our list with no repeated digits is 987, so that is the number we are looking for.

Answer: 987

Copyright © ARETEEM INSTITUTE. All rights reserved.

2. ZIML Solutions

Problem 17 Solution

We can split the figure in (i) two rectangles of length 2 and width 1, (ii) two parallelograms with base 1 and height 6, and (iii) one parallelogram with base 1 and height 5.

Thus, altogether Pierre's figure has area $2 \times 2 + 2 \times 6 + 5 = 21$.

Answer: 21

Problem 18 Solution

Since Rita spent $4890 on stocks when they cost $24.45, she bought $4890 \div 24.25 = 200$ stocks.

Now that they are worth $6250, the price of each stock is $6250 \div 200 = 31.25$ dollars.

Answer: 31.25

Problem 19 Solution

The surface of the triangular prism is made out of (i) two triangles with base 5 and height 12, (ii) one rectangle with length 10 and width 5, (iii) one rectangle with length 13 and width 10, and (iv) one rectangle with length 12 and width 10.

Adding all the pieces together, the triangular prism has a surface area of

$$2 \times \frac{5 \times 12}{2} + 10 \times 5 + 13 \times 10 + 12 \times 10 = 360$$

square inches.

Answer: 360

Problem 20 Solution

From 200 to 299, the digit 2 is used as the hundreds digit 100 times (one for each number); it is used 10 times as a tens digit in the numbers $220, \ldots, 229$, and 10 times as the ones digit in the numbers 202, 212, ..., 292. So, between 200 and 299 the digit 2 is used $100 + 10 + 10 = 120$ times.

Similarly, between 300 and 399, the digit 2 is used 10 times as a tens digit and 10 times as a ones digit, for a total of 20 times.

Thus, the digit 2 is used a total of $120 + 20 = 140$ times from 200 to 400.

Answer: 140

2.8 ZIML May 2019 Division E

Below are the solutions from the Division E ZIML Competition held in May 2019.
The problems from the contest are available on p.75.

Problem 1 Solution
Since the two smallest squares have perimeter 4 and 8, they have side length 1 and 2, respectively. Hence the remaining squares have side length $1+2=3$, $3+1=4$, and $4+1=5$.

Note the perimeter of the figure is the same as the perimeter of a rectangle with sides $3+4=7$ and $4+5=9$. So the perimeter of the figure is $2 \times (7+9) = 32$.

Answer: 32

Problem 2 Solution
Since the number of people that choose mashed potatoes and the number of people that choose mac and cheese are in ratio $3:5$, out of every $3+5=8$ people, 3 choose mashed potatoes and 5 choose mac and cheese.

Therefore, they need to prepare $224 \div 8 \times 3 = 84$ servings of mashed potatoes.

Answer: 84

2.8 ZIML May 2019 Division E

Problem 3 Solution
The average of the five numbers is equal to the sum of all the numbers divided by 5. If Gloria wants the average to be at least 9, then the sum of all numbers should be $5 \times 9 = 45$ or more. The numbers she has on her table so far add up to $10+9+11+7 = 37$, so she should drink at least $45 - 37 = 8$ glasses of water to have an average of 9 or more glasses of water per day.

Answer: 8

Problem 4 Solution
Since Bob is 15 meters ahead of Dylan after running for 5 seconds, Bob can run $15 \div 5 = 3$ meters per second faster than Dylan. This means Bob's speed is $15 + 3 = 18$ meters per second.

Answer: 18

Problem 5 Solution
To figure out how many pizzas Dolly baked, we can work our way backwards. After two hours there were 8 mini pizzas left, which represent $1 - \frac{2}{3} = \frac{1}{3}$ of the pizzas left after the first hour, so there were $8 \times 3 = 24$ mini pizzas left after the first hour. These are half of the mini pizzas that Dolly took out, so she must have brought out $24 \times 2 = 48$ mini pizzas.

Since she ate 2 mini pizzas before taking them out, she baked $48 + 2 = 50$ mini pizzas.

Answer: 50

Problem 6 Solution

The perimeter of her yard is $2 \times (50 + 30) = 160$ yards.

If she uses a piece of fence with length 50 to divide her yard in two rectangles, she would need $160 + 50 = 210$ linear yards of fencing. Is she uses a piece of fence with length 30 to divide her yard in two rectangles, she would need $160 + 30 = 190$ linear yards of fencing.

Thus, the least number of linear yards of fencing she would need to buy to achieve her goal is 190.

Answer: 190

Problem 7 Solution

To be sure to grab a cube (of any color) or a red object, Sally should not grab a green ball.

There are $9 + 5 + 4 + 6 = 24$ objects in total, so the probability of grabbing a green ball is $\frac{6}{24} = 25\%$. Therefore, the probability of grabbing a cube or a red object is $100\% - 25\% = 75\%$. Thus, $P = 75$.

Answer: 75

Problem 8 Solution

Marty has 2 choices for the color of the Sun, 3 choices for the color of the birds, and 3 choices for the fruit trees (either both of them apple trees, one apple tree and one peach tree, or both of them peach trees). Therefore, Marty has $2 \times 3 \times 3 = 18$ possible choices to draw his landscape.

Answer: 18

2.8 ZIML May 2019 Division E

Problem 9 Solution

We can see the four rectangles overlap in a square with side length 2, so we can split the resulting figure in one square with side length 2 and four rectangles with length $8 - 2 = 6$ and width 2.

Thus, the figure has area $2 \times 2 + 4 \times (6 \times 2) = 52$.

Answer: 52

Problem 10 Solution

Since the first digit of the number is 9 and the first two digits give a number that is twice the number obtained by looking at the last two digits, the last two digits are either 45, 46, 47, 48 or 49. (As twice the last two digits must be at least 90.)

Thus, the possible four-digit numbers are 9045, 9246, 9447, 9648, and 9849. Among these, the only number with sum of digits 27 is 9648, so that is our answer.

Answer: 9648

Problem 11 Solution

If it was an English essay, since $2000 = 2 \times 1000$, he would need $30 \times 2 = 60$ minutes to write it. Given that he spends 20% less time writing History essays, he would need $60 \times 80\% = 60 \times 0.8 = 48$ minutes to write his 2000-word History essay.

Answer: 48

Problem 12 Solution

The figure can be split into 5 congruent rectangles, each with area $2 \times 6 = 12$.

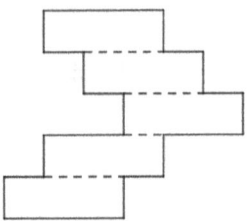

Therefore, the area of the figure is $5 \times 12 = 60$.

Answer: 60

Problem 13 Solution

Since Esteban has visited Taco Bell 48 times since he started collecting his extra sauce packets, there have been $48 \times 50\% = 24$ times he's saved 2 sauce packets, $48 \times 25\% = 12$ times he's saved 1 sauce packet, and $48 \times 25\% = 12$ times he has saved no sauce packets.

Thus, there are $24 \times 2 + 12 \times 1 + 12 \times 0 = 60$ sauce packets in his drawer.

Answer: 60

Problem 14 Solution

From the diagram, we can see that $AB = BC$. So $\angle A = \angle C = 72°$. The three interior angles of $\triangle ABC$ add up to $180°$, so $\angle B = 180° - 72° - 72° = 36°$.

Answer: 36

Problem 15 Solution

We can find the area of each of the three pieces needed to build the house. The base is a rectangle with length 4 inches and width 12 inches, so it has area $4 \times 12 = 48$ square inches. The roof is a triangle with base 16 inches and height 6 inches, so it has area $\dfrac{16 \times 6}{2} = 48$ square inches. The chimney is a trapezoid with bases of length 4 inches and 3 inches, and height 2 inches, so it has area $\dfrac{(4+3) \times 2}{2} = 7$ square inches.

Therefore, the total area of the house is $48 + 48 + 7 = 103$ square inches.

Answer: 103

Problem 16 Solution

If all the popsicles were regular popsicles, there would be exactly 36 popsicle sticks in the freezer. This means the extra $52 - 36 = 16$ popsicle sticks come from the "double popsicles". Since a "double popsicle" has $2 - 1 = 1$ more stick than a regular popsicle, there are 16 "double popsicles" in the freezer.

Answer: 16

Problem 17 Solution

Ron's figure has as many sides as 12 pentagons minus the $2 \times 11 = 22$ sides that were used to glue together the pentagons.

Therefore, the perimeter of Ron's figure is $3 \times (12 \times 5 - 22) = 114$.

Answer: 114

Problem 18 Solution

To be able to have one orange rest on two oranges on the previous row, each row will have one less orange than the previous row. So, the first row will have 12 oranges, the second 11, etc.

Note $12+11+10+9+8+7+6+5+4 = 72$, and $12+11+10+9+8+7+6+5+4+3 = 75$, so 9 rows of oranges would not be enough for all 74 oranges, but 10 rows would be.

Answer: 10

Problem 19 Solution

After the first few jumps the brown rabbit would land on spots that are

$$40, 80, 120, 160, 200, 240, 280, 320, 360, \ldots$$

inches away from the starting point.

After the first few jumps, the white rabbit would land on spots that are

$$30, 60, 90, 120, 150, 180, 210, 240, 270, \ldots$$

inches away from the starting point.

We can see both the white rabbit and the brown rabbit land on the spots 120 and 240 inches away from the starting point. So, they will both visit all spots that are 120 inches away from the previous spot they both visited. That is, they will both visit the spots that are

$$120, 240, 360, 480, 600, 720, 840, \text{ and } 960$$

inches away from the starting point.

Therefore, they both land on the same spot 8 times.

Answer: 8

Problem 20 Solution

The mean of the numbers is $\dfrac{6+4+7+5+7}{5} = \dfrac{29}{5} = 5.8$ and, writing the numbers in order $4, 5, 6, 7, 7$, we can see that the median of the numbers is 6. So the median is indeed larger than the mean of the numbers.

Removing 4 from the list would give us the numbers $5, 6, 7, 7$, so their median is $\dfrac{6+7}{2} = 6.5$ and their mean is $\dfrac{29-4}{4} = 6.25$. So the median is still larger than the mean.

The following table summarizes the possible means and medians obtained by removing one of the numbers from the list.

Numbers	Median	Mean
5, 6, 7, 7	6.5	6.25
4, 6, 7, 7	6.5	6
4, 5, 7, 7	6	5.75
4, 5, 6, 7	5.5	5.5

We can see that if he removes 7 from the list both the mean and the median are equal to 5.5, so that's our answer.

Answer: 7

2.9 ZIML June 2019 Division E

Below are the solutions from the Division E ZIML Competition held in June 2019.
The problems from the contest are available on p.85.

Problem 1 Solution
The perimeter of a rectangle with length l and width w is $P = 2(l+w)$. We know the perimeter of this rectangle is 24, so it must be true that the sum of its length and width is $24 \div 2 = 12$. We know the ratio of the length to the width of the rectangle is $2:1$, so it is $12 \div (1+2) = 4$ units wide and $4 \times 2 = 8$ units long.

Therefore, the area of the rectangle is $4 \times 8 = 32$.

Answer: 32

Problem 2 Solution
During the first leg of the trip the truck traveled at 60 mph for $\frac{1}{3}$ of an hour, so it traveled $60 \times \frac{1}{3} = 20$ miles. During the second leg of the trip the truck traveled at 50 mph for $\frac{1}{2}$ hour, so it traveled $50 \times \frac{1}{2} = 25$ miles.

Therefore, the truck traveled a total of $20 + 25 = 45$ miles.

Answer: 45

Problem 3 Solution
The shaded region is a triangle with base $1+2+3 = 6$ and height 4, so it has area $\frac{6 \times 4}{2} = 12$.

Answer: 12

ZOOM INTERNATIONAL MATH LEAGUE: ziml.areteem.org

2.9 ZIML June 2019 Division E

Problem 4 Solution

To find out how many carrots he had originally, we can work backwards. After eating half of his carrots he was left with 23 carrots, so he had $23 \times 2 = 46$ carrots before that. This amount he had after giving away 20 of his carrots to Loonie, so before he had $46 + 20 = 66$. Lastly, this represents $1 - \frac{2}{3} = \frac{1}{3}$ of his carrots (since he ate $\frac{2}{3}$ of them) so he originally had $66 \div \frac{1}{3} = 66 \times 3 = 198$ carrots.

Answer: 198

Problem 5 Solution

Recall the area of a circle of radius r is $r^2 \times \pi$. Since the area of the small circles is $4 \times \pi$, they each must have radius 2. Thus, the radius of the large circle is $2 \times 3 = 6$.

Therefore, the large circle has area $6^2 \times \pi = 36 \times \pi$, so $K = 36$.

Answer: 36

Problem 6 Solution

Let's give Rollie 5 more treats. This would mean they got in total $29 + 5 = 34$ treats, each of them the same amount. Thus, Petra received $34 \div 2 = 17$ treats last week.

Answer: 17

Problem 7 Solution

The rectangular piece has length 7 and width 2, so it has area 14.

Two of the triangular pieces have base 3 and height 2, so each has area $\frac{3 \times 2}{2} = 3$.

The triangular piece at the tip of the rocket has base 2 and height

2, so it has area $\dfrac{2 \times 2}{2} = 2$.

Therefore, the total area of the paper that Raquel needs to make her diagram is $14 + 2 \times 3 + 2 = 22$.

Answer: 22

Problem 8 Solution

Since we just care about the ratio of the number of pencils, we can choose a convenient number to do calculations. The LCM of 3 and 5 is 15, so let's assume Clara had 15 red pencils and 15 blue pencils.

Clara lost $\dfrac{2}{5} \times 15 = 6$ of her red pencils, so she has now $15 - 6 = 9$. She also lost $\dfrac{2}{3} \times 15 = 10$ of her blue pencils, so she has now $15 - 10 = 5$.

Thus, out of the $15 + 15 = 30$ pencils she had, she has $9 + 5 = 14$, that is, $\dfrac{14}{30} = \dfrac{7}{15}$ of her pencils. Therefore $Q - P = 15 - 7 = 8$.

Answer: 8

Problem 9 Solution

A guest has 3 options for the type of bread, 4 choices for the type of meat, and 2 choices for each of the 4 veggies (put it on the burger or not). So, there are $3 \times 4 \times 2 \times 2 \times 2 \times 2 = 192$ different possible ways to order a burger at Make-A-Burger.

Answer: 192

Problem 10 Solution

The first triangle has base 3 and height 5. So, the second triangle has base $2 \times 3 = 6$ and height $2 \times 5 = 10$, and the third triangle has base $2 \times 6 = 12$ and height $2 \times 10 = 20$. Therefore, the third triangle has area $\dfrac{12 \times 20}{2} = 120$.

Answer: 120

Problem 11 Solution

1 has only one factor. Prime numbers have exactly two factors; among these numbers, 2, 3, 5, 7, 11, 13, 17 and 19 are prime, so each has 2 factors.

The rest of the numbers have more than 2 factors. Since we have checked so far 9 numbers, there are $20 - 9 = 11$ of these numbers that have more than 2 factors.

Answer: 11

Problem 12 Solution

We can fit the kite into a rectangle whose sides are parallel to the sticks (diagonals) of the kite, as pictured on the diagram below.

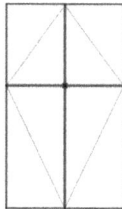

Note the length and width of the rectangle are the same as the lengths of the two sticks used to make the kite.

From here we can see the area of the kite is half of the area of the rectangle. The rectangle has area $3 \times 5 = 15$, so the kite has area $15 \div 2 = 7.5$ square feet.

Answer: 7.5

Problem 13 Solution

In increasing order, the number of pieces of paper he's used over the past seven days is

$$4, 5, 6, 7, 8, 8, 8,$$

so the median of the numbers is the middle number 7. Thus, he will bring $7 + 2 = 9$ pieces of paper with him today.

Answer: 9

Problem 14 Solution

The director has 10 choices for the hero, 9 choices for the first villain, and 8 choices for the second villain. So he has $10 \times 9 \times 8 = 720$ ways to pick a hero, a first villain and a second villain. Since he does not really care who is the first villain and who is the second villain, and there are 2 ways to swap the order of the villains, we need to divide by 2. Thus, there are $720 \div 2 = 360$ different ways for the director to choose the actors.

Answer: 360

Problem 15 Solution

She spent $2.80 + 4.50 + 3.50 = 10.80$ in food. A tip of 20% would be $10.80 \times 0.2 = 2.16$ dollars and tax is $10.80 \times 0.07 = 0.76$ dollars. Thus, Lauren would pay $10.80 + 2.16 + 0.76 = 13.72$ dollars.

Answer: 13.72

Problem 16 Solution

If she paints about 12,000 dots in one hour, after 5 hours she'd have painted approximately $12,000 \times 5 = 60,000$ dots. Since she needs about 200,000 points to finish her painting, she has painted $60000 \div 200000 = 0.3 = 30\%$ of her painting.

Answer: 30

Problem 17 Solution

Ms. Robertson needs to buy $60 \div 12 = 5$ packs of pencils, $60 \div 20 = 3$ packs of erasers, and $60 \div 30 = 2$ packs of pens. Thus, she will spend $5 \times 2.50 + 3 \times 2 + 2 \times 5 = 28.50$ dollars.

Answer: 28.5

Problem 18 Solution

Lance's figure has 16 sides of length 1 and 6 sides of length 2. So the perimeter of his figure is $16 \times 1 + 6 \times 2 = 28$.

Answer: 28

Problem 19 Solution

If we add 4 to Ron's number, it would be a multiple of both 7 and 8.

A number that is a multiple of both 7 and 8 is a multiple of their LCM, 56. The first few multiples of 56 are $56, 112, 168, \ldots$, so Ron's number is one of $52, 108, 164, \ldots$. We see the only number between 100 and 150 is 108, so that must be Ron's number.

Answer: 108

Problem 20 Solution

There are 8 possible outcomes for flipping a coin 3 times:

$HHH, HHT, HTH, HTT, THH, THT, TTH,$ and TTT.

We can see there are exactly 4 outcomes that have at least 2 heads: HHH, HHT, HTH, and THH. So, each of them has a $\frac{4}{8} = \frac{1}{2}$ chance of getting more heads than tails.

Thus, the probability that both of them get more heads than tails is $\frac{1}{2} \times \frac{1}{2} = \frac{1}{4}$. Therefore, $Q - P = 4 - 1 = 3$.

Answer: 3

3. Appendix

3.1 Division E Topics Covered

Note: Setting up and solving equations is not necessary for the problems in Division E (there are rare exceptions among the earlier monthly contests though). Students are allowed to use equations to solve the questions, but the questions are designed to be solved without using equations or systems of equations.

Word Problems

- Calculations and Arithmetic: Adding, subtracting, multiplying, and dividing whole numbers, fractions, and decimals
- Ratios and Proportions: Using ratios to find parts of a whole, Calculating missing information from proportional relationships, etc.
- Percents: Calculating percent increases and decreases, Relationship between percents and ratios, Using percents in mixture problems (e.g. 40% water and 60% oil)
- Problem Solving Methods: Chicken and Rabbit method, Using ratios when given sums or differences
- Motion Problems using (Speed)x(Time)=(Distance), Average Speed, Applying proportions to motion problems

- Work using (Rate)x(Time)=(Work Done), Average Rate of Work, Applying proportions to work problems

Geometry

- Areas and Perimeters of Basic Shapes such as triangles, rectangles, parallelograms, trapezoids, and circles
- Symmetry of Polygons
- Similar Triangles: Equal Angles, Sides are in a common ratio
- Geometric Reasoning with Areas: Congruent shapes have the same area, Dividing a shape and rearranging areas to find patterns, etc.
- Volumes and Surface Areas of Basic Solids such as cubes and rectangular prisms (boxes)

Number Sense

- Place Values: Ones/units digit, tens digit, hundreds digit, etc.
- Fundamental Definitions: Quotients and Remainders, Prime numbers, Factors (Divisors), Multiples, Perfect squares, Perfect cubes, etc.
- Least common multiple (LCM), Greatest common factor or divisor (GCF or GCD)
- Sum and Product Rules for Counting
- Sequences: Arithmetic and Geometric Sequences, Sum of elements in an arithmetic sequence, Finding patterns for general sequences
- Probability: Gives the chance of something happening, Ratio of outcomes
- Basic Statistics: Mean (Average), Median, Mode for lists, Interpreting data from graphs, bar charts, tables, etc.

3.2 Glossary of Common Math Terms

Acute Angle An angle less than $90°$.

Altitude of a Triangle A line segment connecting a vertex of a triangle to the opposite side forming a right angle. Also called the height of a triangle.

Angle A figure formed by two rays sharing a common vertex. Often measured in degrees.

Arc The curve of a circle connecting two points.

Area The amount of space a region takes up. Often denoted using square brackets: area of $\triangle ABC = [ABC]$.

Arithmetic Sequence A sequence where the difference between one term and the next is constant.

Average See Mean.

Base of a Triangle One side of a triangle, often used when the altitude is drawn from the opposite side to this base.

Chord A line segment connecting two points on the outside of a circle.

Circle A round shape consisting of points that all have the same distance (called the radius) from the center of the circle.

Circumference The perimeter of a circle.

Composite Number A number that is not prime.

Congruent Two shapes or figures that are exactly the same.

Cube A solid figure formed by 6 congruent squares that all meet at right angles.

Deck of Cards A standard deck of cards has 52 cards. There are 4 suits (clubs, diamonds, hearts, and spades) with each suit having cards of 13 ranks (A (ace), $2, 3, \ldots, 10, J$ (jack), Q (queen), and K (king)).

Denominator The bottom number in a fraction.

Diagonal A line segment connecting two vertices of a shape or solid that is not an edge of the shape or solid.

Diameter A chord passing through the center of a circle. The diameter has length that is twice the radius.

Die or Dice A standard die (plural is dice) has 6 sides. Each of the 6 sides has the same chance when the die is rolled.

Digit One of $0, 1, 2, \ldots, 9$ used when writing a number.

Distinguishable Objects Objects that are different.

Divisible A number is divisible by another number if there is no remainder when the first number is divided by the second. For example, 35 is divisible by 7.

Divisor A number that evenly divides another number. For example, 6 is a divisor of 48. Also called a factor.

Edge A line segment connecting two vertices on the outside of a shape or solid.

Equally Likely Having the same chance of occurring.

Equiangular Polygon A shape with all equal angles.

3.2 Glossary of Common Math Terms

Equilateral Polygon A shape with all equal sides.

Equilateral Triangle A regular triangle, one with three equal sides and three equal angles.

Even Number A number divisible by 2.

Exponent The number another number is raised to for powers. For example, in a to the power of b (a^b), the exponent is b.

Face The shape or polygon on the outside of a solid region.

Factor of a Number A number that evenly divides another number. For example, 6 is a factor of 48. Also called a divisor.

Factorial The symbol ! where $n! = n \times (n-1) \times (n-2) \cdots \times 1$.

Fraction An expression of a quotient. For example, $\frac{1}{2}$ or $\frac{9}{7}$.

Geometric Sequence A sequence where the ratio between one term and the next is constant.

Greatest Common Divisor (GCD) The largest number that is a divisor/factor of two or more numbers.

Greatest Common Factor (GCF) See Greatest Common Divisor.

Indistinguishable Objects Objects that are the same.

Isosceles Triangle A triangle with two equal sides and two equal angles.

Least Common Multiple (LCM) The smallest number that is a multiple of two or more numbers.

Mean The sum of the numbers in a list divided by the how many numbers occur in the list. Also called the average.

Median The number in the middle of a list when the list is arranged in increasing order.

Midpoint The point in the middle of a line segment.

Mode The number or numbers occurring most often in a list of numbers.

Multiple A number that is an integer times another number. For example, 72 is a multiple of 8.

Numerator The top number in a fraction.

Obtuse Angle An angle between $90°$ and $180°$.

Odd Number A number not divisible by 2.

Parallel Lines Lines that do not intersect.

Perfect Cube A number that is another number cubed. For example, $64 = 4^3$ is a perfect cube.

Perfect Square A number that is another number squared. For example, $64 = 8^2$ is a perfect square.

Perimeter The length/distance around the outside of a shape.

Pi (π) A number used often in geometry. $\pi = 3.1415926\ldots \approx 3.14 \approx \dfrac{22}{7}$.

Polygon A shape formed by connected line segments.

3.2 Glossary of Common Math Terms

Prime Factorization The expression of a number as the product of all its prime factors. For example, 24 has prime factorization $2 \times 2 \times 2 \times 3 = 2^3 \times 3$.

Prime Number A number whose only factors are one and itself.

Proportional Ratios Ratios that have equal values when expressed in fraction form. For example, 2 : 3 is proportional to 8 : 12.

Quadrilateral A shape with four sides.

Quotient The integer quantity when dividing one number by another. For example, the quotient of $38 \div 5$ is 7 as $38 = 7 \times 5 + 3$.

Radius of a Circle The distance from the center of the circle to any point on the outside of the circle.

Randomly Chosen for a group of objects. Unless specified, the chance of choosing each object is the same as any other object.

Rank of a Card See Deck of Cards.

Ratio A relation depicting the relation between two quantities. For example 2 : 3 or $\frac{2}{3}$ denotes that for every 3 of the second quantity there are 2 of the first quantity.

Rectangle A quadrilateral with four right angles (an equiangular quadrilateral).

Regular Polygon A polygon with all equal sides and all equal angles (equilateral and equiangular).

Remainder The quantity left over when one integer is divided by another. For example, the remainder of $38 \div 5$ is 3 as $38 = 7 \times 5 + 3$.

Rhombus A quadrilateral with four equal sides (an equilateral quadrilateral).

Right Angle A 90° angle.

Right Triangle A triangle containing a right angle.

Scalene Triangle A triangle with three unequal sides and three unequal angles.

Sequence An ordered list of numbers.

Similar Shapes or solids that have the same angles and sides that share a common ratio.

Square A shape with four equal sides and four equal angles (a regular quadrilateral).

Suit of a Card See Deck of Cards.

Surface Area The total area of all the faces of a solid.

Trapezoid A quadrilateral with one pair of parallel sides.

Triangle A shape with three sides.

Vertex The intersection of line segments, especially the intersection of sides or edges in a shape or solid.

Volume The amount of space a solid region takes up.

3.2 Glossary of Common Math Terms

With Replacement When choosing objects with replacement, a chosen object is returned to the others allowing it to be chosen more than once.

3.3 ZIML Answers

ZIML October 2018 Division E

Problem 1:	2913	Problem 11:	12
Problem 2:	13	Problem 12:	40
Problem 3:	201	Problem 13:	84
Problem 4:	36	Problem 14:	7
Problem 5:	42	Problem 15:	14
Problem 6:	7	Problem 16:	27
Problem 7:	2	Problem 17:	63
Problem 8:	115	Problem 18:	10
Problem 9:	34.3	Problem 19:	0.27
Problem 10:	4	Problem 20:	219000

3.3 ZIML Answers

ZIML November 2018 Division E

Problem 1:	1.6	Problem 11:	20.64
Problem 2:	26	Problem 12:	32
Problem 3:	120	Problem 13:	3
Problem 4:	80	Problem 14:	66
Problem 5:	1200	Problem 15:	98
Problem 6:	85	Problem 16:	87
Problem 7:	12	Problem 17:	31.7
Problem 8:	4.8	Problem 18:	108
Problem 9:	60	Problem 19:	6
Problem 10:	8709	Problem 20:	6

Copyright © ARETEEM INSTITUTE. All rights reserved.

ZIML December 2018 Division E

Problem 1:   250

Problem 2:   1200

Problem 3:   20

Problem 4:   43

Problem 5:   9

Problem 6:   2

Problem 7:   50

Problem 8:   63

Problem 9:   50

Problem 10:   80

Problem 11:   64

Problem 12:   216

Problem 13:   8

Problem 14:   19

Problem 15:   3

Problem 16:   27

Problem 17:   141

Problem 18:   16

Problem 19:   139

Problem 20:   23

3.3 ZIML Answers

ZIML January 2019 Division E

Problem 1:   6

Problem 2:   41

Problem 3:   27

Problem 4:   162

Problem 5:   37

Problem 6:   62.5

Problem 7:   84

Problem 8:   6

Problem 9:   90

Problem 10: 1300

Problem 11: 26

Problem 12: 25

Problem 13: 16

Problem 14: 8

Problem 15: 4800

Problem 16: 101

Problem 17: 7

Problem 18: 18

Problem 19: 16

Problem 20: 96

ZIML February 2019 Division E

Problem 1:   28

Problem 2:   6

Problem 3:   4320

Problem 4:   180

Problem 5:   56.67

Problem 6:   11

Problem 7:   52.5

Problem 8:   44

Problem 9:   30

Problem 10: 21

Problem 11: 68

Problem 12: 49

Problem 13: 21

Problem 14: 279

Problem 15: 21

Problem 16: 29

Problem 17: 1314

Problem 18: 27

Problem 19: 21

Problem 20: 264

ZIML March 2019 Division E

Problem 1: 20

Problem 2: 11

Problem 3: 27

Problem 4: 248

Problem 5: 9

Problem 6: 5

Problem 7: 8

Problem 8: 15

Problem 9: 96

Problem 10: 584

Problem 11: 8

Problem 12: 10

Problem 13: 172

Problem 14: 23

Problem 15: 36

Problem 16: 42

Problem 17: 4410

Problem 18: 3

Problem 19: 47

Problem 20: 86

ZIML April 2019 Division E

Problem 1: 15

Problem 2: 4

Problem 3: 93

Problem 4: 11

Problem 5: 117

Problem 6: 2

Problem 7: 5

Problem 8: 105

Problem 9: 2

Problem 10: 222

Problem 11: 13

Problem 12: 72

Problem 13: 13

Problem 14: -384

Problem 15: 9

Problem 16: 987

Problem 17: 21

Problem 18: 31.25

Problem 19: 360

Problem 20: 140

3.3 ZIML Answers

ZIML May 2019 Division E

Problem 1: 32

Problem 2: 84

Problem 3: 8

Problem 4: 18

Problem 5: 50

Problem 6: 190

Problem 7: 75

Problem 8: 18

Problem 9: 52

Problem 10: 9648

Problem 11: 48

Problem 12: 60

Problem 13: 60

Problem 14: 36

Problem 15: 103

Problem 16: 16

Problem 17: 114

Problem 18: 10

Problem 19: 8

Problem 20: 7

Copyright © ARETEEM INSTITUTE. All rights reserved.

ZIML June 2019 Division E

Problem 1:   32

Problem 2:   45

Problem 3:   12

Problem 4:   198

Problem 5:   36

Problem 6:   17

Problem 7:   22

Problem 8:   8

Problem 9:   192

Problem 10:   120

Problem 11:   11

Problem 12:   7.5

Problem 13:   9

Problem 14:   360

Problem 15:   13.72

Problem 16:   30

Problem 17:   28.5

Problem 18:   28

Problem 19:   108

Problem 20:   3

www.ingramcontent.com/pod-product-compliance
Lightning Source LLC
Chambersburg PA
CBHW071204160426
43196CB00011B/2196